Dear God,

Is This You?

To Ann—
May these bring joy to your days,
stimulate your mind
and make your spirit soar!
Kit Inman

Dear God, Is This You?

Finding God in unexpected places and glimpsing Him in eternal, infinite spaces

Kit Inman

ISBN : Softcover 1-4010-6838-3

This book was printed in the United States of America.

To order additional copies of this book, contact:
Xlibris Corporation
1-888-795-4274
www.Xlibris.com
Orders@Xlibris.com
16019

Contents

CHAPTER II

CHAPTER III

CHAPTER IV

CHAPTER VI

CHAPTER VII

INTRODUCTION

This book is dedicated to the glory of God.

If man's goal in life is getting to know and serve the One living and loving Lord God Almighty, this book of poems and meditations reflects my growing awareness of andcommitment to Him.

From the wonder of His created world, little and large, its intricate beauty and design, to the joy of His presence, to the failures, questions and complaints, I poured out my soul in words. As my faith grew and strengthened, the wonder expanded. How can mere man grasp omniscience, omnipotence, agape love, infinity and eternity? We can receive, but how can we comprehend salvation, forgiveness, being in Christ, and the indwelling Holy Spirit? And Why is there the eternal fight between good and evil, Satan and God. Why do we have free choice? Are heaven and hell real? How can Jesus and His Word be one? What a wonderful, incomprehensible God we worship!

The more God reveals of Himself to us, the more we realize how little we know, and the more eager we are to know more. It will take eternity to satisfy that yearning.

ACKNOWLEDGEMENTS

Many friends, my family, Bible Study and art students have given me invaluable feedback. They have persuaded me that these records of my joyful realizations of the wonders of God, of my struggles with the challenges of God, and the insights He has given me, will help others in their journey with our loving Lord. Thank, you, every one for years of loving encouragement.

Kit Inman

Chapter I

Dear God, How Could You Create This Wondrous, Complex World?

1. Rainbow Harvest

Today I found a crop of dew
Full ripened in the morning light,
A little field of softest green
Sprinkled with sun, full of flowers of bright.

Yesterday the grass was there,
Carefully tended, full and trim,
But in the night the rain and air
Sneaked the buds of moisture in.

Miraculously, the crystal buds
Burst open, as I turned my head,
Into rainbow sparkles, changing
From purple to blue to yellow to red.

Praise, praise! All praise to You,
Creator and Essence of purest Light,
For giving me this glimpse of You
In this rainbow harvest of sheer delight.

2. This Instant

You knew I'd be here at this instant, Lord,
And prepared this beauty for me:
A feast for my eyes, a joy in my heart,
Your love in a red autumn tree.

3. Ripples

One small stone dropped in a pond
Sends rippling circles extending.
One kind word dropped in a crowd
Ripples kindness in circles unending.

4. Maple Seeds

So many maple seeds, Lord,
All over the grass, the sidewalks, the streets,
Washed down drains by the rain,
Does the maple tree despair at the futility?
No! It claims fertility.

So many words, oh Lord,
From my lips, from my heart,
Proclaiming life eternal,
Telling of Your love,
Seeking to plant Your redeeming Truth
Into one soul of fertile ground!
And so many turned away in disdain,
In polite love, seeking not to offend,
Or, unheard, swirling away into silence in the air!
Shall I despair at the futility?
No! I shall claim fertility
For my words, so long as they are Thy Words.

In my garden this spring,
I find baby maple trees.
In Paradise, O Lord,
I shall find souls
Won by Your planted Word.

5. Husbandman

As sprinkled water quickens grass,
As hedges greedily absorb its flow and grow,
So is Living Water of the Spirit to my soul.

As fertilizer in prepared soil to petunias,
As nutrients in tilled ground to peaches,
So is the Word to my Spirit.

As cultivation, weeding, pruning, loving care
Enhance the thoughtful choosing and planting
Of God's created and nurtured wonders,
So prayer and meditation enhance my faith.

Let me not be a careless husbandman
Of Your eternal Truth and infinite grace.
Let my heart be fertile, prepared soil
For the seed of Your glorious Word,
That I may bring forth much fruit
And scatter seed bounteously
In fields Your Spirit has prepared.

6. Lessons

Little leaf, teach me how to live.
You receive from branch, trunk, and root
Your life-giving water;
You turn toward the light of the world

For your creative power,
Using that light to grow, produce, and share.
With your brothers, you bow to the mighty wind,
Or dance, fluttering in joy,
Or hold tight to your branch in storms,
Content to be utterly dependent on your source
And even in dying, glorify your Maker
With blazing color.

Tall tree, teach me of your Maker.
Your life began with a seed,
Holding all your completed fullness.
Patiently you grew day by day, year by year,
Into your planned pattern for unknown purpose.
Your life's work was to receive air, water, light,
And change them into leaves, wood, and fruit,
To make seeds for more trees like yourself.
Was it hard enduring drought, storms, and attacks?
Was it hard to let go of leaf, fruit, and seed?
Do you fear dying, trusting your seeds for your eternity?
Tall tree, is there no Jesus to die for you?

7. From Wonder into Wonder

The step from matter-of-fact acceptance
Into wonder is the start:
That a flower can be so lovely,
That there's music in the brook,
That the stars are ever there (where?),
That there's love, and one can care.
From wonder into wonder,
Think on these things.

Step from wonder into understanding,
Of seed to flower to seed,
Like producing like in certain and infinite variety,
Of similitude of sound and light in waves,

And pictures of sound in electronic patterns,
Of suns and planets, comets and galaxies,
Quasars, black holes, and white giants,
Of philosophy and psychology
And man's basic need of love,
From wonder into wonder,
Think on these things.

Grow in understanding
Of the why's and how's,
Laws and patterns,
The eternal rhythms and provisions
Of atoms and nature and universes,
Of light and life and love,
Of interdependence and relationships,
Of origins and annihilations,
Of powers and The Power,
From wonder into wonder,
Think on these things, in awe.

For if we find not God in our thinking,
We cannot grow in wisdom and knowledge
Beyond the limits of time and space
Into the eternal and the infinite.
We cannot see the Creator's plan
In the awesome multiplicity of things
Created from faith by the Word.
But we can fit into His perfectly prepared plan,
Channeling God's power to work His will,
Bringing the Creation into the Creator's order,
And finding there His love, joy, and peace.
From wonder into wonder,
Think on these things.

And when we enter into eternity,
And see without the darkening glass
The wondered mysteries of all infinity unfolded,

Whether we sit in Christ at the right hand of God,
Or separated forever in the despair of hell,
How much more will we wonder
As we think on these things?

8. Fall Housecleaning

The trees are doing their fall housecleaning,
Gathering the precious green of life together,
Storing it in the cellar, protected, until spring.
But before they store their life forces
Of sap and chlorophyll,
They plan their spring color scheme,
Place their blueprints and designs
For all their spring decorating and summer tasks.
They position the seeds for their fruit,
Programming each bud for leaf or flower,
On hold, ready to be empowered.
Only then do they give away used clothing
To the wind, or soil for protection or nutrients.
Twigs and limbs, empty of life-giving sap,
Are ready for ice, winter storm, and March winds
To prune and decorate.
All prepared, sap warm under the earth,
The tree sleeps.

We, too, need to let go of last summer's worn ideas,
Separating the living from the dead,
Releasing the dead, no matter how lovely,
And preserving the living, the essence of life,
To prepare the new and living sprouts,
Leaves and fruit for our Lord's harvest.
We need to wait patiently through cold winter storms,
Ready for pruning,
Content with our bareness,
Stripped of camouflage,

Waiting to bring forth new life for our Master,
Eagerly awaiting the life-giving Son,
Savoring His Light,
Joyfully, faithfully responding
In life and growth.

9. Birdbrain

So tiny the head of the mocking bird
That his brain has become a mocking word.
He sits as if thinking on the high wire,
But how much of a brain does he require?

And yet, can micro-circuits men train
By using their God-given brain
Form a computer that small
Which can also do it all—
Find and recognize food?
Make a home that's good?
Feel the cold and fluff its feathers?
Seek shelter and shade in adverse weathers?
Recognize danger and flee
To a safe house-top or tree?
Find his own kind for a mate,
And not only procreate
But feed the fledglings in the nest
And push them out when that is best?
Protect them with menacing dive,
And for them even with a man strive?
Know which man he can trust
And fly away from the rest of us?
Return every spring for years?
Imitate any bird call he hears?
Hop, and fly, and soar?
Can man's tiny computer do more?

Sums, products, square roots, per cent
Are solved because numbers are set
In rigid patterns by God's own rule,
But can a computer find its own fuel?
Can it determine what problem to do?
Can it use its wisdom for itself, too?
Can it reproduce, or just multiply?
Can it live, and sing, and fly?

10. Mission Accomplished

My flower box lives on borrowed time
But blooms in bursts of joy,
Ignoring frost on open lawn
And future cold that will destroy.

It has shared its summer beauty,
Formed and ripened seeds to scatter:
Bonus days for a little more sharing—
It's the seeds with new life that matter.

We redeemed are living on borrowed time,
Kept alive by the Spirit within,
To share blossoms of joy and love
And spread seeds of the Word for Him.

11. Little and Large

Oh, Lord, I marvel at the meticulous perfection
Of Your little things:
Sun-sparkled rainbow in a raindrop
Hanging on a twig,
Or in a prism, or diamond;
Lacy geometry of a snowflake;
An electron in orbit ready to define

The identity of an atom,
Or sail off to make another atom;
A white corpuscle armed for battle;
A DNA molecule with its secret formula
For freckles or mathematical genius;
The miracle of chlorophyll
In one tiny leaf-cell or plankton
Uniquely designed to translate
Sunlight into solid energy;
A spark to start a warming fire—
Or a Holocaust;
An invisible sound wave
Identifiable as my loved one's voice
Or as a musical note, or an alarm;
A predictable pink petunia seed.
Oh, Lord, I marvel at the meticulous perfection
Programmed into the littlest parts
Of Your perpetual creation.

Lord God Almighty,
I wonder at the awesome grandeur
Of Your large creations:
Oceans and mountain ranges,
Redwood forests and deserts;
Weather cycles with their prevailing winds
And seasons from Your orbit tilt;
The drawing of the earth to moon in tides
As the moon circles, held securely by its earth;
Your systems, Lord,
In man, nature, mathematics, space—
Exceeding computer wonders,
Never failing, never lacking;
Your suns with their comets, planets, moons and meteors;
Galaxies expanding, white giants and black holes;
And the unknowable, anticipated wonder
Of infinity and eternity
With the miracle of our inheritance in them.

Lord God Almighty,
I wonder at the awesome grandeur
Of Your creations, large and little,
And the oneness of them,
United in systems, patterns, purpose,
Each reflecting Your magnificence,
Your infinite love,
Each leading, as we probe its depths,
To You, Creator of each part,
And essence of the whole.

12. Lover

As the lover woos his lady
With pre-planned, joyous surprises,
With the perfect red rose,
With the flawless jewel,
The meticulously planned picnic;
As the lady woos her lover
With eye-appealing gown,
Carefully arranged hair,
Fragrance and grace,
Cookies and pie,

So have You, Lord God Jehovah,
Wooed Your beloved man
Throughout the ages
With pre-planned joyous surprises:
With the red-orange dawn
Filling the hemisphere
Changing to half a sky of yellow,

Then flashing a rainbow across the sky,
Or tucking it in a raindrop,
Perfuming the soft, blushing rose petal,
Or hiding buttercups and dandelions in the grass,

Varying apples from tart to sweet, red to green,
Changing seasons like stage settings,
White to green to flaming red and gold,
And filling the air with music
From streams, birds, wind and waves,
Sparkling and spreading sunlight on everything
Each flash creating its own beauty;
Warm sun, cool breezes, refreshing rain,
And more and more and more—
You have loved us from before creation,
In this very beauty-filled moment,
And into eternity.

Oh, Lord, may we recognize the unsigned Giver
Of each lovely extra in our world,
And seeing in the wonder of each gift,
The wonder of Your love.
Always, may we accept the Giver with the gift.

13. Wise As a Cabbage Seed

How wise the cabbage seed!
It doesn't need a mother to instruct,
A father to discipline.
It knows how to grow:

To push down roots for water,
To stretch up shoots for sun.
It is never double-minded, or ambitious—
Straining to be broccoli, or cauliflower.
It never misses its mark;
It never worries, or hurries,
But in fullness of time forms its head.
It never complains of sun, heat, or late rain,
Or when it is cut down before
It can flower and make seed.

Lord, teach me to be wise
As the cabbage seed.
My new spirit You carefully planted
In the heart carefully prepared
By Your Holy Spirit.
You offer the water of Your Living Word,
The nurturing of prayer,
Your unfailing presence.
Let me never worry or hurry, nor wonder—
Just put my roots deep into that Living water,
And help me grow up high into the Son,
Never questioning, never doubting
That in the time of harvest
My seed will have produced fruit
Just as the Master planned—
In His very image.

14. Prepare Ye the Way

As the sun sends forth
Gentle whispers of its coming,
And the soft violins of pinks,
Joined by the bold reds of trumpets
Preparing the way for his entry,
And from his early presence
Touches leaves and windows,
Lakes and puddles,
With bright orange glow,
Later brightening the view with light gold,
And then revealing every wonder and detail
In floodlight of full day,

So does the Son send before His coming
To the seeking heart,
The faint, gray rumors of possibility,
Brightening into the pink of hope,

Bursting out in the red blaze of faith,
Bringing in the dawn of new life.
And every familiar leaf and pebble,
Every drop of water is golden in His light.
It brightens with the growth of knowledge
Which increases to Truth in the Light of His wisdom,
With wonder in every detail.

And is the floodlight of His Word
And the joy of His presence
Just the faint messenger
Of the wonders awaiting us
In the brilliant beginnings
Of our eternity in the presence of our God?

15. How Odd

How odd that sounds would fall into patterns
Of octaves and harmonies,
Recognizable whether made by accident or nature,
By rock striking rock or water falling,
Or wind rustling trees, birds calling—
Recognizable, reproducible
With voice or man-made instruments!

How odd that light would bend into colors,
With natural compliments and combinations,
Recognizable, reproducible, usable!
How odd that the speed of light is so constant
It becomes our measuring stick!

How odd that radio and ultrasonic microwaves
Fit into unity with sound waves man can feel,
With all related to light, that all can be focused
Into tools of power and communication,
Predictable, measurable, but limitless!

How odd that the stars follow patterns
Moving in measurable speed and direction,
And that planets, moon, sun and stars
Set our seasons in precise perfection!

How odd that the sun activates our weather,
Drawing up water, creating winds to blow clouds,
In jet streams and hurricanes,
Forming breezes and rain.

How odd that gravity draws rain to the sea,
Yet holds in place not only stars and planets,
But also man and electrons!

How odd that elements fall into tables,
Each with its own number and characteristics,
Weight, complexity, and predictable combinations!

How odd that seed reproduces after itself,
Never into any other form, recognizable
Even with subtle differences within.
How odd that thirty or more can write 66 books
Over thousands of years in separate times,
And all be one in thought and theme,
Presenting a God Who never changes,
With a Truth that stands the tests of ages,
With laws that cannot be improved,
With a love that cannot be denied,
With a plan for mankind that cannot be thwarted!

How odd that man would search for ways
To explain away the Creator of all this order!

16. The Gardener

Forty years of rewarding toil accomplished,
My husband is planting fruit trees.
(Lord, You are planting fruit trees, too.)

Carefully selecting his choice varieties,
(Lord, You have selected me)
He is preparing hole-y ground by digging deep,
Removing the unyielding clay,
And filling in humus and topsoil for a bed.

When the trees arrive, roots bound,
He will open the ball and set them free,
(Christ, You have set me free.)
And spread them lovingly into their prepared place.
He gently covers them with enriched soil,
Waters and firms them once again.
(You have planted me by Living Waters, Lord.)
Then he fertilizes them
To erase studied deficiencies and provide food.
(Feed my spirit with Your Living Word.)
He will prune the branches drastically
To remove all unprofitable growth,
Training the tree to grow straight and strong
(Sometimes the pruning hurts, Lord.)
He protects by spraying to eliminate
All harmful pests and diseases.
(You have given me Your shield of faith,
Helmet of Salvation, Breastplate of Righteousness.)

And then we will wait, my love and I,
Sharing hopes and dreams in anticipation.
(You are patient, Lord.)
Through the seasons, through the early years
He will watch over his trees with loving care.

(You never sleep, O Lord.)
He checks the bark for the green sign of life
Watching for buds to swell,
Eagerly celebrating the first leaves,
Savoring the delicate blossoms with joy.

His heart will rejoice with the first fruits
Which he will bring me as loving gifts.
(Do You rejoice as we give first fruits to You?)
Together we will enjoy the fruit of his labors,
Faithfully tending and receiving
The bounty of God's creation in action,
And gladly sharing with friends and neighbors.
Nourished, the tree will reveal
The miracle of air and water and chemicals
Growing into delicious food
According to God's law and Providence for us.
As we tend the tree,
As God provides the sun and rain,
The tree just grows where it is planted,
Producing fruit because it is its nature.
(Lord, may I grow where You have planted me,
Producing fruit to Your glory and good pleasure.)

17. God's Prism

In the searchings of my heart,
And in the exquisite joy
Of Your presence, Lord,
I pray for You to show me
How I can share Your eternal love,
Your mysterious peace and joy,
The wonders of Your created world,
And let others glimpse
Your Truth, Your Power, and Your glory.

If these poems are answers to my prayer,
Let me not quench the flow;
Let me not mar Your purpose
With my fumbling words,
Nor dim Your understandings
By interposing my own.

Let these poems be clear as glass—
No, let me aspire to more—
Let me be a prism to scatter
Your rainbows that Your will be done.

The joy, the unutterable joy,
Oh, Lord, to be Your Prism.

Chapter II

Dear God, Is This Love, Joy, and Peace from You?

1. I Heard Your Whisper

I heard Your whisper
In the prism rainbow, Lord,
Spread in glory on my table by the rose,
And stepped a moment out of time and space
Into our meeting place in anywhere,
And always faithful, You were there.
Pleased that I heard and came to You,
In that untimed moment You circled me in love
To hold and fill and lift as long as memory.

Greedy, I wanted more, so You pressed my hand
Through the sparkly rays
Around the reflected sun in the curved glass dome.
I closed my eyes to hold
Your brightness in my heart,
And heard again, "Go ye unto all the world,"
And, "Lo, I am with you always."
When I opened my eyes, Your sparkle
Had slipped away into dull wall and memory.

Dear Lord, the more You send Your love,
The more I want.
The more time I spend with You in love and prayer,
The more I want to linger there forever.
And when, no longer hindered by mortality,
I stand a timeless eon before Your throne,
In love and wonder, prayer and worship,
Will I still long for more?
Is all eternity enough to be with You?

2. Moments of Joy

One flaming maple leaf centered in my doorstep,
Left by wanton wind, or by one who shares
The upsurge of joy in beauty perfectly positioned;

Or by one who painted the fiery undercoating
Long ago last spring in patient anticipation
Of autumn unveiling;

Or by One Who programmed long ago last fall
A bump of bud on a branch to swell, unfold,
And spread its factory green camouflage
Until time for delivery on my doorstep;

Or by One who implanted
In the first created maple seed
Millions of moments of flaming joy
Pulsing in multiplying circles,
Perfectly positioned in infinite, eternal variety.

Lord, my soul praises You.
Thank You always for parading moments of joy
Overflowing my heart.

3. Guardian Angel

You have a guardian angel
—maybe three or four—
And he'll protect you in the roughest times.
That's what God sent him for.
God loves you. Can you guess how much?
More, a hundred times more!

4. God Loves Us

God loves me! Yes, I know it's true!
He sent me a dear friend like you
Who rejoices with me as we share
The insights He gives us, and every care.
Who in my every need is with me there
To meet with Him in deed and prayer.

He chose you, you know—hand picked for me,
And He chose me for you—it's plain to see.
I thank our God for endless lists
Of provision, blessings, and Covenant gifts.
God loves us; yes, we know it's true!
What joy to be in Jesus, up close to you!

5. God's Peace

God's peace does not depend on men,
On ended wars or settled strife,
On safer streets or loving homes,
On health, wealth, or success in life.

Peace comes from knowing He is God,
That He cares so much for me
That for my sins His own Son died,

To heal my illness and injury.

He comes especially when I'm still,
Meditating on His Word,
Holding my wishes to His will,
Acting when His voice is heard.

6. Rose-Colored Glasses

I'm looking at the world
Through rose-colored glasses,
Learning the joy of seeing through love,
The peace of choosing, like my Lord,
To look through the blood-tinted lenses
Of forgiveness, long-suffering, and meekness.
No blinders or distortion—
I'm observing the world's evil and rebellion
Through the Truth of God's Word,
But delighting to gaze with faith
Beyond the obvious to the hope of answered prayer,
Through the power, provision and promises
Of my Lord and God.
I'm looking at the world through rose-colored glasses,
Looking at you through rose-colored glasses.
All thanks and praise to Almighty God
Who looks at me through rose-colored glasses,
Through the precious blood-tinted glasses
Provided by His eternal love and grace
According to His plan before the world began.
He sees me redeemed, righteous, blood-washed,
Completed through His grace.
He sees me walking in His calling,
Obedient to His will and Word.
I know the ugliness inside,
And so does He, more than I.
Yet instantly, when I repent and ask,

Blood-bought forgiveness, rose-colored glasses!
With joy and peace He places me through faith
Inside His Son, my Lord and Savior.
In Him, He sees me through His blood shed for me,
Looking at me through rose-colored glasses.
All of the sin of the world in all of time
Was paid for with the blood.
Yes, my sin and yours.
Already God is seeing you with love and longing
Through rose-colored glasses.
The moment you accept your Lord and Savior,
He sees you in His Son, forgiven and free,
Through those precious blood-tinted,
Rose-colored glasses. Hallelujah!
You, too, will be looking at the world,
At friend and foe, and even at me,
Through rose-colored glasses.

7. Woo Me with Beauty, with Joy

Spirit God Almighty, how do You find ways
To love your creatures, to woo them
From dead spirit in dying flesh
Into eternal spirit full of promise?

Do You woo us with beauty, Lord,
So exquisite that our hearts lift
Beyond the creation to the Creator?
Oh God, Who is Spirit,
Woo me with a rainbow,
Win me with a rose!

Do You woo us with Joy, Jehovah?
With unexpected moments
When our hearts on tip-toe
Recognize the perfect harmony

Of every sense and truth,
And in one incredible instant know the Source?
Touch me with a bright, soaring bubble;
Show Yourself in the silver edge around clouds;
Hold me with baby hand around my finger,
        and my heart.
And when we are Yours, Dear Father
Of our Lord and Savior, Brother and Friend,
Do You talk to us of love
Through beauty, through joy?
Is this how you make Your love tangible?
How can we press Your hand
To let You know we recognize Your touch?
How do we show You that we love You, too?
Do we send beauty and joy
Into another heart in Your name?
Do we touch a hand to transfer
Your love through us?
Bake a cake for a new neighbor?
Give a coat to a cold child?
Send Your Word by radio to a hungry people?
Oh, Lord, may the You in me
Share love and beauty and joy in Your name;
May I love You by loving Yours.
Jesus, touch my heart with joy,
With a soap-bubble rainbow.
Teach me to pass on Your joy
Through a note or a song or a rose,
And receive it back through a touch,
A smile, a word, a gift—
All the time knowing that the joy is You,
And that You share the joy shared.
Keep loving me with joy, Oh Father God,
And show me how to love You back with joy.

8. Living Trust

I'm setting up a living trust,
Investing for eternity,
Tax-exempt, inflation-proof,
With God as my security.

A tenth of income I should include,
And add a tithe of time,
Plus sharing of the eternal Truth
In teaching and in rhyme.

Ready prayers for hurting souls,
With love, and listening ear,
And sharing goods with hungry men
Whose needs are now and here.

I'll add total commitment to my Lord,
Obedience to His will,
Faith in His Word, incessant prayer—
The investment is paltry still.

I'll choose my Savior as Trustee,
And put all in His loving hand,
Confident of heavenly return
When in His presence I stand.

9. A Place for Me

Lord God Jehovah,
In Whom we recognize the ultimate
In power and wisdom and righteousness,
Lord God Creator,
Who encompassed all history into Your plans,
Set in motion all laws and systems
Adequate for time and for eternity,

Lord God our Lord,
Setter of standards and Judge,
Teacher and Guide and King,
Does Your perfection include openings?

For You are Father, loving and merciful,
Understanding and forgiving,
Caring enough to be hurt or angry,
Patient in leading us to Your high standards,
And You are Friend,
Waiting for us to come to You in love
To share our dreams and moods and praise,
Longing for us to come to You.

Does perfection include
Deliberate incompleteness
To open a place within Your infinite greatness
For our love, praise and fellowship?
Are we, Your new creations,
Conceived out of a cosmic loneliness
For freely offered fellowship
Throughout eternity?

10. Measure of Truth

With our world so full of fascinating facts,
Mysteries, imaginations, and lies,
Seeking Truth is our life-long task;
Using Truth well will mark us as wise.

How can we know what is Truth, what is not?
We use our faith as a measure—
Beginning with trust in touch, ears and eyes,
Letting parents' faith judge trash or treasure.

Horizons expand to neighborhoods, schools,
With bushels of claimed facts to sort
From teachers and friends, wise ones and fools;
Growing faith and doubt test each report.

How sad when we learn we cannot trust
All people, books, TV values and news,
For much truth is distorted through
    choice or chance,
And what man believes true shapes his views.

We may have a phase where the cynic is wise,
And he who believes is a fool.
Above the world's negatives, faith will arise
To provide a more accurate tool.

Ever and always, Truth is illusive,
And our faith is like shifting sand
Until we meet the Proof conclusive
And commit to His heart and hand.

The measure of faith grows strong and true
As we hear the unfailing Word.
Our knowledge increases, and wisdom, too,
Bearing witness to Truth we have heard.

In Christ as our Savior, Lord, and King,
We find of all Truth the essence.
Faith in Him and His Word can always bring
The true measure of all the world presents.

With a universe full of fascinating facts,
Mysteries, imaginations, and lies,
Christ calls us to our lifelong task—
With His saving Truth we're to open blind eyes.

11. Target

In the vast, empty reaches of space,
Does not the sun shine?
Do not light waves and heat waves flow?
Yet space is cold and dark.

But God has hung a world in place,
A substance for the rays to find,
To warm the air, to make grass grow,
A target for His living spark.

Without a world to warm and light,
The sun's rays have no work to do.
What sadness if God's love had found
No place to rest and light in you!

12. Giving Yourself Away

You came, Lord Jesus, the Living Word,
To give Yourself away,
To share Your love, Your joy and peace,
Your wisdom and strength, Your Way.

You showed us the Father and His love,
His desire to share His eternal life,
The creative longing to perfect
His dear creation, marred with strife.

You called me, Lord, to follow You,
To give myself away
In Your love, Your joy and peace,
Your wisdom and strength, Your way.

So I've shared Your Word, dear Jesus,
To anyone who'd come;
I've blown rainbow bubbles of poems,
And painted Your creation for some.

But have I followed You, dear Lord?
Or have I missed Your call?
Were rainbow bubbles meant for floors?
Paintings more needed for wall?

You've given me too much to share
For me to hold it in;
I'd burst if I couldn't give it away,
So it must not be a sin.

You're awesome, wonderful Jesus,
And the whole world ought to know
Of Your gifts of love and eternal life.
We need to tell them so.

13. What Can We Love?

What can we love?
Can we love a pizza?
A rose?
A sunset?
A home?
A country?
We're coming closer.
A dog?
A baby?
Our mate?
Our child?
God?
Not until the "what" becomes a "who"
Can we dignify our emotion as love.

God created—and called His creation good—
But only man does He love.
He so loved the world—the people—
That He gave His Son.
Christ did not die for roses,
Or for sunsets or trees or mountains,
But for you, for me, for men and women,
One by one.

God is love, and love is giving
Some precious time or strength or value,
Something of ones self—
As God gave His Son, His only begotten Son—
For the good of another.
Not to stop the baby from crying,
Not to get loving in return,
Or be called great, good, or generous,
But that whosoever believeth on Him
Shall have everlasting life!

Where do we find love?
In God.
When we open our hearts to Him,
His infinite love flows in,
Overflowing in unselfish caring for another,
Giving of ourselves for His sake,
Enjoying every moment of it,
For the more we share, the more God fills,
And we can never outgive God
(Or outlive God)
But we can live forever with Him
Loving,
Giving,
Receiving love to give again.

14. I Need to Be Still

I need to be still, and let God love me.
When this old world starts to roar and shove me,
I need to be still, and let God love me.
I need to relax, and let God take over;
To let God take the load off my shoulder.
When there are troubles all around me,
And my soul cries out for rest,
When I feel as if I'm failing,
Even though I've done my best,
When decisions get too heavy,
And there are answers that I seek,
I need to be still, and let God love me.

15. The Ultimate Valentine

Dear Lord, each year about this time
When love is put in rhyme,
My heart is increasingly aware
Of love overflowing to friends everywhere.

I think of shining eyes,
And see Your love in every one.
I remember joys of giving
And sharing hours of fun.

But as I grew in understanding
Of the wonders of Your love,
I realize that all the love I feel
Is abundance from above.

I love so much my heart nearly bursts
With fullness of this wonder—
That You love me even more than this!
What blessings we are under!

You've shown us what love is all about,
And yet we still are learning,
And as You teach me through Your word,
To love like You is all my yearning.

I love You, Lord, with all my heart,
And You assure me Your love is mine.
Would it be impudent to ask
That You be my Valentine?

16. When Soul Discovers Soul

What joy when soul discovers soul
Through open, loving eyes,
Probing the depths and truth within
To admire, accept, and sympathize.

What joy to share with unchained words
Common hopes, dreams, and fears,
Appreciating differences,
And pledge faith throughout the years.

What joy encircled in loving arms
As the two become as one
In holy, sanctioned ecstasy,
Knowing as they are known.

What joy when a soul discovering God
Invites Jesus to be His Lord,
Welcomes His Holy Spirit within,
And is filled with His love and His Word.

17. Love Around the World

I send help and love around the world,
Hoping some will hear
For since Jesus filled my heart with love
It spreads from here to there.

That's how God loves: so much, so strong,
That He sent His Son to die,
To pay the penalty for our sin—
That we may love forever, you and I.

If we believe in our hearts, confess with our mouths
That Jesus is Savior and Lord,
We'll live with Him eternally—
He's promised it in His Word.

18. Sending Love

Of course I want to send you my love—
Any day, every minute, for it is there—
But something in me rebels at salesman's pitch,
At easy sentiment on display everywhere.

Easy sentiment, easy love, easy words—
They've stolen the heart's sincere confession,
But then, am I any more sincere in my words?
Do I add my deeds to my love-expression?

Let me find the moments in busy days
To write, to visit, to share,
And show you, my friend, without a word,
That you're my friend, and I care.

For once we experience the love of God,
Giving, demanding no thing in return,
There's so much love piled up in our hearts
That giving it to friends—for that we yearn.

19. God's Valentine

This Valentine Day I'm not speaking for me;
(Although that I love you is true),
I've a message for you from Love Himself.
He wants you to know He loves you.

"Have you not heard?
Can You not see?
The love my child gives you
Is really from Me?

"I long to make you mine,
To live in your heart,
To place you in My Son
So we'll never have to part.

"I've proven My love by paying the price,
For redeeming you from sin.
Accept My gift of My precious Son:
Open up your heart and let Me in.

"If you'll meet with me each day
In worship, praise and prayer,
I'll lead you safely in the Way
And carry your every care.

"I won't love you just one day,
Or just when we agree;
I'll give you infinite love
For all eternity. Free!"

Chapter III

Are You Really with Us All the Way?

1. Time for Me

In His eternity where time flows free,
My Father God has set aside for me
Abundant, infinite time, high quality.
He waits, and longs for me if I delay,
Delights when I am bold to claim His Way,
Repentant, expectant, faithful every day.
He never hurries, worries, or turns aside
To other prayers or cares while I abide,
But treasures our time together, nor derides.
He listens lovingly to every care,
Forgives each sin, and answers every prayer.
I thank Him, worship, praise, and feel Him there.
In His eternity, there's always time for me.
My Father God invites me into His infinity.

It's equally, eternally, awesomely true:
Our Father has infinite time, too, for you.

2. You Are There

You are there—everywhere,
You're aware; You care.

You are near, and we hear,
"Do not fear; I am here."

3. Holding Hands

In the invisible world of the atom,
Where a raindrop is formed
By elements holding hands
In planned patterns,
Where the atom itself is formed
By energy in motion
In planned patterns,
Pushed in place by some unseen hand,
Where would the water be
If the atoms dropped their handholds?
Where would the atom be
If God dropped the faith-hold?
In the invisible world of faith,
Where the Body of Christ is formed
By Christians entering into the Spirit world
Into the Body of our Lord Jesus Christ
And holding hands, united by our love,
Where would we, the Body, be
If you no longer reach and hold my hand,
Nor I, my brothers?
Where would we be, you and I,
If the faith that holds the life
In our new-born spirits were gone,
Eliminating the energy of that life?
O Lord, keep Your faith in force,
Upholding all things by the Word of Your power,
Uniting elements into matter
With hand-holds of harmony!
O Lord, keep us alive with faith in motion,
And together in the Body of Your Son,
Holding hands with the power of love.

4. Keeper of the Keys

Boxes, rows and rooms and worlds of boxes,
Lavish in decorations of ideologies,
Encrusted with jewels of ideas,
Bright colors of gaiety and pleasures,
Sex goddesses and bas-reliefs of great men
Carved masterfully to entice,
And barely visible within the lure
Of gold or fame or lust or rest—or hopelessness—
Boxes set as snares for us,
Beautiful, intricate traps.

But once we enter, accepting as our goal
The gold or fame or lust or rest,
The box closes, and we are trapped,
Into one lifetime ending with a death—
One lifetime without God.
The Spirit in us struggles to climb out,
To breathe the air of hope,
But locked in our atheism,
We drag it back to smother,
Or slam down the lid to amputate.

All glory to Thee, Oh God,
Who has the key to every box of Satan,
Who knows the reality of the Spirit,
Recognizes each struggling soul
Gasping and pushing and straining to escape,
And waits only to be asked
To open and set free.

5. Altogether Lovely

Altogether lovely, are You, Oh Lord,
Altogether wise and knowing,
Altogether mighty and powerful,

Altogether righteous,
Altogether forgiving and merciful,
Altogether faithful,
Altogether true.

Altogether all that is wonderful and fine—
Creator, Judge, Father,
Savior, Lord, Son and Brother,
Friend, Comforter, Guide, Teacher—
Altogether God Almighty,
Father, Son, and Holy Spirit,
All together One, Eternal, Infinite,
All together.

6. Horizons

Lord, keep our horizons wide and deep,
Measured by Your infinity,
As vast as mind and feet can keep,
As love can touch, as wonder see.

Should faltering steps limit our world,
Let us see more clearly in the near
The miracles in Your creation curled,
Evidences of Your presence here.

If eyes and ears and friends should fail,
Let us fellowship with our God inside,
Content that Your love and joy prevail,
Treasuring the Word in which we abide.

Keep our horizons wide and deep—
As the eternity where our souls reside,
Alive and alert until we sleep
To awake upon the other side.

7. Miracle-Working God

Our God is a miracle-working God,
On duty night and days
In unexpected ways,
Watching His faith and power in His Word
With our speaking the Word we've heard.

Watch for the miracles of our God
In coincidences and happenstance,
In doors opened or closed, in generous grants,
In delightful moments of unexplained joy,
In the peace that nothing can destroy.

Expect the miracles of our God
Each time your needs go up in prayer;
In difficult times, look for Him there.
Never too soon, never too late,
He gives more than you anticipate.

Wait for the miracles of our God,
For His time is better than our goal,
And faith with patience enriches the soul.
He uses the waiting for preparation,
Rewarding faith with celebration.

Thank God for the miracles of our God,
For His love, omnipotence, and grace,
For salvation, and our eternal place.
Be so sure of His Word and loving care
That you thank Him before the answer's there.

8. Heaven Is Where You Are

Sometimes I picture You on Your throne in Heaven,
Brilliant with glory,
Circled by the rainbow of promise.

The four living creatures
Are crying, "Holy, Holy, Holy,"
And a myriad of angels singing "Hallelujah!"
With thousands of redeemed worshipping You
On the sea of glass before Your throne.
And I am there.

Sometimes I crawl up on Your lap
And rest in the eternity and infinity
Of Your love and peace.

Sometimes You walk with me
In the beauty of Your creation
Sharing the wonder of Your Word,
And You open to me the deep things of God,
Or in the dark storms you lead and protect me,
And hold my hand.
Sometimes I kneel at Your feet
In my prayer closet.
(You are always there.)
I seek forgiveness, search Your Way,
Ask questions, share needs, intercede,
Thank, worship, and praise You.

Sometimes I find you right inside my heart,
Comforting, teaching, guiding, correcting,
And always loving me.
When Your people meet together expectantly
In praise, You are always within the circle.

Sometimes, in willful rebellion,
I try to hide in myself or in the world,
But I sense Your presence,
And peek through my fingers,
To see You smiling, arms open wide.
I repent, and rush to get inside.

Our Father, Who art in heaven,
You are there, and everywhere,
For there is no distance in infinity,
No time in eternity.
You are always at the point of need,
And if that isn't heaven, it is heavenly.

9. "Let Go"

Keep Him Who is Lord of Lords and King of Kings
Lifted up, for He is worthy.
Only then will you reach your fullness.
Lift up your hands, people of God,
And praise the Lord Your God and Your Savior.
Nation, lift up hearts in praise,
And our God will lift up our nation.
The world is waiting for America
To lift up our hearts and hands in praise.

"Let go, My children. Let go
Of all the old ways, all the hang-ups,
And rest in Me.
You are My children
And I am in control of your lives.
For this is the desire of your hearts
Since you have committed yourselves to Me.
Do not fret that there are still imperfections:
I see you completed.
In My time, I will take care of each flaw.
Yield yourselves and your nation
Into My hands, for I love you,
And I direct the paths of the yielded ones
Whom I have chosen. Be patient.
You are in My will; You are Mine.
I have chosen you."

10. Infinite

Our God is infinite. There is no limit
To His Love, His Power, His Wisdom, His mercy,
His Joy, His Strength, His Peace, His Justice,
His Righteousness, His Light, His Word,
His Abundance, His Holy Spirit.
There is enough and to spare.

There is enough for us, and to spare,
As much as I am willing to receive,
As much of His Love, Power, Wisdom, Mercy,
Light, Word, Justice, Abundance,
Of His Holy Spirit,
So much will He give to me, or to you.
There is always more:
The more I give away, the more He gives.
And He is not diminished by His giving—
And I am not diminished by my giving.
Our God allows us to be an outlet for His infinity.

There is enough for our world, and to spare.
As many as come to Him will be filled,
Filled with His Love, Power, Wisdom Mercy,
Light, Word, Justice, Abundance,
And His Holy Spirit . . .
As much as they are willing to receive,
And our world can be an outlet to the universe
For His infinity.
And the universe will not exhaust God's infinity.

God's caring is infinite, too,
And not only infinitely large,
But infinitely small,
Small enough for the tiniest crack
Into the tiniest heart

Of the tiniest part of His infinity,
As much, or as little as the heart will receive,
To grow and overflow,
To draw that heart into His infinity, His eternity,
For another outlet to other hearts.
Our God is infinite.

11. How Patient You Are!

Oh Holy Spirit, how patient You are!
Dear Holy Spirit, living in my heart,
Ready, eager, yearning to empower God's Word
As I in obedience feed on Him,
Digest Him, meditate on Him,
As I, in growing faith, speak the Word,
Live the Word, share the Word.
Oh, Holy Spirit, how patient You are!

How great a love and longing
God, our Father, has for His children, even me!
How great a price our Lord Jesus Christ
Has paid for us to be new born!
How great a sacrifice You are making,
Dear Holy Spirit, to come to live in us, even me!

You humble Yourself to live in me,
Releasing Your power, working in me
According to my obedience
In feeding on the Word to mature in faith,
According to my knowledge of the Living Word,
To my listening to Your patient guidance,
To my releasing Your prayers through my lips,
To my yielding my will to Yours,
To my willingness to speak and do the Word.
Oh, Holy Spirit, how patient You are!

You, the Power of the Universe,
Are coiled in the Word
Waiting for my heart to recognize,
My lips to release,
My body to act in faith
Oh, Holy Spirit, how patient You are!

Forgive me, Holy Spirit
For the barriers I put in Your way,
For willful ignorance, doubt, murmuring,
For relying on reason and feelings
Instead of the Word.
For reading superficially
When I should be meditating on the Word,
For talking when I should be listening,
Even in prayer,
For failing to recognize Your guidance
In prayer, in fleeting thoughts,
For wallowing in self-pity,
Or plodding on my way in pride
Instead of asking for Your help.
Do I hinder my prayers
With my negative confessions?

Forgive me for the Word not spoken,
The prayer not prayed,
The prompted deed not done,
Faith not exercised.
Why do I live in weakness when You are in me,
Eager to empower the Word
Boldly spoken in faith?
Oh, Holy Spirit, how patient You are!
And yet, oh Holy Spirit, You are in me,
Ready and able to comfort, teach, guide,
and empower me
In Christ, the Living Word.

You are in the Body of Christ
Waiting to be sought,
Acknowledged, authorized, released,
To bring into reality
The fullness of the kingdom of God.
Oh, Holy Spirit, how patient You are!

Oh humble Holy Spirit.
Power of the Universe waiting,
How patient You are!

12. Circle of Giving

Our Father is a giving God,
Eternally pouring out His infinite gifts
Of Love and Light and Life,
Power and plenty and pity,
Works and Wisdom and the Word of Truth,
Even sharing His glory.

Our Jesus is a giving God
Offering His life and death as channels
For God's gifts to reach to every man,
So that every man may reach God.
As God gave His love to Jesus,
Jesus gave it back to God and on to man—
No problem: infinite love multiplies infinitely.
God, essence of Light, gave His Light
To Jesus, as the Light of the World,
And Jesus plants in us that wondrous Light.
God, Who is Life, through Jesus gave us Life.
All power God gave to Jesus
Who gave to us that power in His name.
Does any man lack wisdom?
Let him ask, and it is his.
God gave the Words to the Living Word

Who gives the Living Word to us.
God gave His Holy Spirit in fullness to His Son
Who gives to His who ask the Indwelling Spirit.
Those works God gave to Jesus to perform,
Jesus commissioned us to do, and greater.
God not only gave again His glory to His Son,
But the Son won again man's original glory
And offers it again to us.
Are we, His Church, a giving family of God?
As we receive in faith each divine gift,
Let us pass it on three ways:
Upward to God in thanks and praise,
Outward to each other,
And on to those bound in the world
To free and bring their new-born, living souls
To God, as gifts of gratitude for our freedom.
Let us gladly receive and use each glorious gift
For the Givers' glory.
For we, chosen by God before the world began,
Ourselves are gifts from God to Christ,
From Christ to God and to ourselves
That we may be set free,
And rejoicing in faith,
We give our new-born selves to Christ, to God,
Casting our crowns of glory at His feet,
Unending circle of giving.

13. Rescue Mission

Father:

Son, our created men are lost in sin.
Will You go down and bring them in?

Son:

Father, whatever You will is my will, too.
We love them so. What must I do?

Father:

Remember our plan before time began?
You'll be born of a virgin, become a man,
Resist Satan and flesh, live a perfect life
Of love and service, overcoming strife.

Son:

In so wicked a world, with perfection Your
  demand,
How will I as a man be able to stand?

Holy Spirit:

God will send Me, His Spirit, to live in You,
To show you each word, each deed to do.

Son:

If I die for sin once, I can't do it again.
How will salvation spread to all men?

Father:

When Your time comes,
I'll place on You all sin,
And You'll die in man's place,
And rise again.
You'll teach a few men
The Word of Faith for rebirth,
Save them with Your death.
And through them the whole earth.

Son:

Against Satan, the world, and the flesh
Men are weak.
How will born-again men
Find the strength they seek?

Holy Spirit:

The Father will send Me to live inside;
They'll have the power of Your name,
And in Your Word abide.

Father:

In the fullness of time, I'll send You back, Son,
To claim Your bride, to live here as one.

Son:

And after Satan is thrown in the Lake of Fire,
We will finally see our eternal desire:
A new heaven and earth cleansed of all sin,
With Our redeemed with us eternally within.

14.The Wonder of It All

The wonder of it all!
That life can survive
In a seed, in a bulb—
Through airless cold
And dry months or years,
And still be alive,
Still be itself,
Never another species.

The wonder of it all!
That dead dirt,
Inanimate air,
The chemistry of water,
And warmth and light can encourage
Life from a seed or bulb!

The wonder of it all!
That in created dirt,
Created life,
Plus the air of the Holy Spirit,
Plus Living Water of the Word,
Plus the warmth of Love,
Plus the Light of the World
Bursts out in new Life in a soul!

The wonder of it all!
That man can be so blind
To the Creator of the seed,
The Creator of the soil,

The Holy Spirit in the air,
Christ in the Living Water of the Word,
Almighty God in the Light of the World,
To the Truth that God is Life!
The wonder of it all!

15. Beginning Math, According to God

When my mother and father were one,
Then there was me, and we were three.
Yet the two that were one were in me,
And I was in one.
And the oneness of my mother and me,
Became two, and I was one.

I met my husband, and we were two,
But became one.
I met my Lord,
And He invited me into His heart,
And I invited Him into my heart,
And we two became one.

But the one with my husband,
And the one with my Lord
Split in two—
That wouldn't do!

So I prayed to my Father, and He agreed—
Sealed in His Word—
That my husband and I who were one,
Were also one with our Lord,

And we who were three
Are now one in unity.

16. Answered Prayer

I prayed for angels on the way—
Before, behind, beside, above, below—
In Jesus' name I bound the troublemaker,
Casting out disease and pain
In me and my loved ones
Coming, abiding, and going,
All the time, all the way.
In His Name I called the cars sound,
Forbidding breakdowns or trouble.
I asked a blessing for the house,
Love, joy peace, harmony and oneness.

They laughed.

But plans were altered—
One family leaving a day early,
One an hour early, and deciding
Not to stop for the night,
All three precious carloads arrived safely
Before the winter storm,
Before the closing of the road on Christmas Eve.
I thank my God for answered prayer.

Coincidence, they claim.

A perfect visit—love, joy, peace and harmony.
Even the children played in joy, peace, and love.
The house was warm, beds snug,
Outings pleasant, parking spaces open,
Lines short, interesting and informative sights,
Weather lovely, gifts enjoyed, tasks shared,
Health abounding in all.
I thank my God for answered prayer.

"Weren't we lucky this time?" they said.

One precious family safe at home tonight,
Winding the two-lane mountain road
With nothing more than white knuckles.
(If they had believed in the angels, not even that.)
Another will be home tomorrow
With no mishap, no sickness or pain.
The plane to California and back
Will fly my son protected, safely home.
I thank my God for answered prayer,
And thank the angels for fulfilling God's Word
As I released it in faith.

Dear Father, open their spiritual eyes
That they might see Your faithfulness,
That they might know Your love,
That they might realize the angels are there,
That they might believe in answered prayer.
I thank You, Father, for answered prayer.

17. In Me, In Him

Me—afraid and proud,
Hurting and rebellious,
Lonely life-of-the-party,
Carefully kind and generous,
Selfishly careful and prudent,
Foolishly wise, willfully ignorant,
Wildly stubborn,
Childishly curious—Longing, seeking, denying rejecting,
Cracking and closing doors—
Me, needing HIM.

Him—loving and patient,
Waiting my invitation,.
Caring that I hurt,
Longing to help,
But honoring my choice.

What is so great about an independent life?
What treasures am I so reluctant to lose?
If I'm such a great captain of my soul,
Why am I dashing against rocks in this storm?
If I ask HIM in . . .

In me, like a cup of water in a parched mouth,
Like the candle in the fuse-blown house,
Like detergent in the greasy skillet,
Like Brahms replacing acid rock,
Order out of chaos,
Fine-tuning away of blurred images,
Sense out of confusion,
Peace out of turmoil,
He is in me, and I am changed, made new.

In HIM, I let Him take my sins, my sufferings;
In Him, I see Him suffer for me.
Safe in Him, I accept His death for mine;
Alive in Him, I die,
And for an instant grasp the hell
That should be mine,
And in Him rise again,
Completely new, completely alive.
Washed clean with His blood,
Clothed in His righteousness,
I find myself in Him seated
At the right hand of His Father and my father,
Worthy because I am in Him

To live instead of die,
To receive the wondrous gifts
Our Father ordained for us,
To use the Name above all names,
To live in the Living Word,
To serve and witness and overcome
In Him.

18. Empty Cross

Empty cross,
Empty tomb.
        He's alive!
        Forever alive!
And in Him, where He is,
With our Father in heaven,
We too shall live.

20. Rescue Mission II

God sent His Son to earth
To rescue his fallen man:
His death and resurrection
Carefully planned before Time began.
Christ Jesus is coming again
To rescue His church
From the Day of the Lord,
Out of calamity into His eternity.

21. The Only Way

Almost two thousand years have passed
Since that awesome Revelation was written:
God's judgment on a wicked world.

Has God changed His mind about sin?
Has His love and mercy for His imperfect man
Lessened the penalty of death for lies,
For unrepented adultery and homosexuality?

In His Word He said, "I am the Lord; I change not."
And, "No man is righteous, no not one."
And, "The wages of sin is death."

But yet, He has also said that He
"So loved the world that He sent
His only begotten Son, that the world
Through Him might be saved."

And the Son told us in His Word,
"I am the Way, the Truth, and the Life;
No man cometh unto the Father but by me."

Is there, after two thousand years,
Another way?
Was that horrible death on the cross
Unnecessary?
Has God decided that good men of any faith
Are worthy of His heaven?
Without Christ?
Has He changed His definition of sin?
Is repentance enough without accepting Christ?
Or is modern man simply trying to remake
God in a kinder image to allow for sin?

If God is indeed eternal and infinite,
Creator of time and space, and man,
His Word, too, is eternal and does not change.
Today, as always, Jesus is the Way,
The only Way to eternal life.

Chapter IV

We're Struggling; Are You Here?

1. Dismal Days

I tell others to put on the garment of praise
For the spirit of heaviness,
But the praise is choked in discouragement,
Though my soul knows I am blessed.

I teach tearing down of strongholds,
But my self-pity builds a wall,
And I am just too tired to fight the mood
With Your Word that conquers all.

I struggle to seek Your kingdom first,
But my husband rejects my priority,
So I work with things and study finance,
And life is heavy without Your joy.

Lord, carry me through these dismal days,
For I know You are with me now and always.

2. Sixty Is a Hill

Sixty is a hill for looking back—
It all looks so flat!
Where are all those mountains
I thought I'd climbed?
Those valleys that stretched
Dark hours and miles?
Lord, it's such a little hill.
I'd like to climb one mountain.
Is sixty, maybe, half-way up?

3. Delete

Once spoken, a word forever remains.
We cannot take it back;
For good or evil,
It echoes through eternity.

Once done, a deed makes its mark
On our lives, in lives of others,
For good or evil,
Forever done.

How can we erase that word regretted?
How can we undo that careless deed?
By tapping some cosmic computer key
Can we delete? Erase the memory?
And the consequences?
Oh, would that we could!

We cannot, but God can.
He has given us the way
Through His eternal Word
That nothing can erase or delete.
With that powerful Name of Jesus,
Given to us who are His,

Those words can be rebuked,
Forgiven, though consequences remain.
Those deeds can be forgiven,
Erased from the eternal record
Of our Father.

Praise God for providing
That key to delivering deletion.
Our screen is cleared in Heaven
Of all our errors lifted up to Him.

4. Detours

So many things that must be done,
And hours, though endless, could drift away
In detours of memories, roadblocks of tears,
Or plod in low gear through the cluttered days.

But there is One Who plans our paths,
Who helps and guides us ever true.
We know the joy of His promises,
And hear Him say, "I am with you."

5.Like a Vacuum

Like a vacuum, my dear one, you are pulling me
Back into the blackness of the world—
There is nothing there for me.
I cling to my shallow prayers—
Why are they so shallow
When the depths in me cry out for God?
I try to praise, for the garment of praise
Overcomes the spirit of heaviness.
I cling to the Word, for I know
That the Word is powerful and true.
But in the world, praise is hollow.
The world spurns the Word.

Dear one, why do you want me to go back?
There's no life in the world,
Only death—spiritual death.
I do not fear physical death,
But the blackness of a Godless world
Closes in on me.
Dear one, why don't you give a place to God,
A place for Him to live in your heart,
So that we could live together in Christ?
It's so much better than the world.
Dearest God, don't let me be sucked up
Into the blackness of the world.

6. Submission

Born again a bright blue butterfly,
I spread my wings with joy unspeakable,
Sipped nectar from the Word and prayer,
Teachers, and fellowship.
I spread His Word and love
From flower to flower
Until at last I heard the oft-repeated Word,
"Go back to your cocoon and wait
Until released to fly by your mate.
You can find joy and nectar there
For I am with you everywhere."

On fire with the Light of the World,
Filled with the oil of the Spirit,
I set my lamp on a lamp stand,
Eager to shine, to show the Way.
Firmly He placed me back within the walls
To brighten the home alone
Until my husband also bids me shine abroad.

Filled with Living Water from above,
I longed to be a fountain to the thirsty,
To pour out rivers to encourage life,
Constantly replenished with the Living Word.
Although I tried, I could not ignore
The dam of submission,
The faucet of obedience,
Nor let the Living Water flow in tears,
For I must quench the flow in joy.

Oh Lord, I long to fly, to shine, to flow,
Encouraged by Your will in Your inspiring Word;
If waiting now is better, let me know.
My will is obedience to Your will as heard,
But still in my heart is the command to go,
And feed the soul of the caged bird.

7. Dandelions

Dear Lord, help!
I know by my little hurts and resentments,
By my hopeless desires,
That I am not yet dead to self.
I have not yet learned to love
As You love me,
Demanding nothing in return.
I have not yet learned to be pleased
In trying to please in patient uncertainty.
My lips have learned to be silent;
My mind has learned to measure by Your Word.
But the battered ego still struggles.
The tears rebel, and the hopes,
Like dandelions improperly pulled,
Push up again and again,
And dying, scatter seeds.

God, I need some weed-killer.
I remind my soul "You are greatly blessed,
Your cup runneth over;
My God is sufficient for all your needs."
I tell my self-pitying self, "You are dead."
I am a new creature, and heaven is my home.
My only goal is to serve my God;
My only praise, the Christ in me;
My only reward, His greeting me with,
"Well done, good and faithful servant."

"Foolish self, do not seek attention,
Approval, appreciation or praise in this world."
Father, I am Your child. The Lord is my Lord.
In His presence is fullness of joy.
His joy is my strength;
His love is my treasure;
In obedience is my peace.

8. Darkness in Light

"God is light, and in Him
Is no darkness at all."
Oh, yes, but Adam who walked
In the light, did fall.
And Lucifer, angel of Light,
Son of the Morning, did rebel,
And men who should know
The God of Light, do go to hell.

God, Who is Light, created
Darkness as well as light—
The Creator is not His creation;
Evil is never right.

But evil is in this world
So that man may have a choice,
And every man decides to answer
Flesh, Satan, or God's voice.

God assures me that Christ is in me,
The Light of the world I must be,
Then why do I sin?
Because He also created me free.

Born in Adam, I live
In an imperfect shell
In an imperfect world
With an adversary of sin as well.

What is the darkness in the Light?
It's not the perfect Light,
But ignorance, weakness of flesh,
Laziness, blinded sight.

The Light within is strong enough
To overcome every sin,
And with His help the dark in us
Is overcome by the Light within.

9. Ghosts

All you dear and precious children
Who pretend on this one night
To be witches, ghosts, or goblins,
Remember, wrong is never right.

I pray angels will go with you,
And Jesus guard your heart
Against wicked thoughts and spirits
Which seek in you a start.

For all the evil spirits
Who try to win your soul
Must one day bow to Jesus
Who is the Lord of all.

10. Simplify

The almighty, infinite, eternal God,
Who is Light and Life and Love,
Reaches out to us in infinite patience,
Teaching us in simplified truths,
Repeated in variation and examples.

Father, What is infinity?
Child, learn to know space and matter, my creations;
Learn to know a grain of sand, a drop of water, a bubble,
And as you study them you will see Me
As Rock, as Living Water, as the breath of Life,
And glimpse the mystery of infinity.

Father, what is Eternity?
Child, consider Time, light years and star charts,
Years and days, hours and seconds—
Then study the moment
Which is the only reality of time.
Learn to live fully in that moment
By yielding it fully to Me,
And I will show you eternity.

Father, what is Light?
Child, I am Light.
Learn the rainbow spectrum,
Learn the power of the sun's rays,
Meditate on lasers and light years,
Wonder at photosynthesis,

Chart the water vapor through the weather cycle,
Probe the sources of all energy,
Learn from the inner light of understanding,
From my Son, the Light of the World,
And you will see Me,
And know me as Light.

Father, what is Life?
Child, I am Life.
Seek to know Me, in My Son,
And you will have Life everlasting.
In Me is all you need and all you need to know.
I have provided a place for you
In Me through My Son, your Savior and Lord.
He is the answer to all your questions;
He is the Way, the Truth, and the Life.

11. Which Way?

Oh Lord, I know You are the Way,
And obedience is my desire,
But when one Word blocks another,
For extra guidance I inquire.
Your Way, dear Lord, is not man's way:
I need not understand, just obey,
But, Lord, of all Your hundreds of commands,
Is there one for women only
That supersedes the others?
May I not go to all the world
And preach the gospel if my love says "stay"?
Or give in the measure of my heart if he says "keep"?
Nor join in joyful fellowship that He disdains?
Nor feed on the Word when he seeks the world?
Nor even be unhappy in restraint,
But in love and joy and faith
Serve within an unbeliever's limits
Until You, my God, through him release me?

Dear Father, Whom I love with all my heart,
Subdue the doubts.
Show me that this one command is from You,
Not the adversary's snare to block the Word,
But Your divine order to discipline me,
And teach me love and obedience.

If obedience to this one command
Releases me from Your orders
If my husband disdains them,
Please give me peace in disobedience to You
Commanded by obedience to my husband.
Oh, Father, this one command
Comes against my yearning to obey.
Are women to screen Your Word
Through husbands' eyes?
Must I place his unbeliever's will
Between Yours and mine?
Shall I accept his will as Yours?
It doesn't seem the same.
Which way, Lord?
Is submission obedience?

12. Don't Sell Your Freedom

Precious, despairing young men and women,
Why do you sell your freedom so cheap?
It was bought for you at a terrible price—
Beatings and sit-ins, insults and deprivation,
Long hours and long years of labor,
Studies squeezed into weary midnights,
Prayers and patience, heroes and martyrs.

Thousands have died to set you free—
In a war between brothers,
War for Independence from tyranny,
Magna Carter and Luther's 20 points,
Even God, God as man, dying on the cross—
All these to set you free,
Free from bondage of slavery and sin,
Free to choose right over wrong,
Free to choose life over death,
Eternally.

And you sell it before you know its worth
For a momentary surge of pleasure,
For a counterfeit sense of power in a gun,
For lust that fools you as love,
For your own way—to what? (You don't know.)
You fill your mind with anger and despair,
With sensuousness and violence,
With hate and hopelessness, empty pride,
And rebellion—against what? For what?
(You haven't yet learned the meaning of life,
The joy and discipline of reaching good goals,
Of helping others find the way of wisdom.
You do not understand that life is eternal,
Both the one from which He set you free,
And the one He died to offer you for free.)

Whatever the temporary thrill of evil,
It isn't worth the sacrifice of freedom,
Because whatever emotion or habit we cannot resist
Becomes our master.

Precious, despairing young men and women,
Don't sell your freedom for a drug,
For lust, for an illusion of power or pride,
For revenge, anger, resentment, or hopelessness.

Freedom, like its Giver, is the pearl of great price,
Costlier than gold, more beautiful than diamonds.
When you learn what freedom is,
When you know the One Who set you free,
Then you will want to offer it to Him,
And be forever free indeed.

13. Whirlpool

In daily nothingness, the world pulls me
Around and around like a whirlpool,
Down, down into the depths of worthlessness.
The negatives of news puncture hope;
Unfinished tasks taunt me.
Age tugs at my ambitions,
Aches and pains sap my will,
While ridicule of my faith tempts me
To crawl into a protective shell of silence.

The ways of the world offer no joy;
The circus of lust and violence, greed and games
Appalls me.
The tyranny of things threatens me.
Deceived by desire to please, to win my loved one,
I submit, suppressing the very Word that is my life.

All wisdom is in Your Word, dear Jesus,
All power in Your Name, my Lord Christ Jesus,
Which You have authorized me to use.
Dear Father, You have given me all spiritual blessings
In Christ Jesus, Your Son, my Lord.
All Your promises and commands
Open and outline the Way.
Precious Holy Spirit dwelling within me,
You alone can teach me the Way.
Lead me by Your voice.

My loved one, in the world, does not have the answer.
If I accept his answers, his goals,
The whirlpool claims me.
Only You, dear Lord, are the answer.
The enemy tries to distract me
From my hours of refreshing,
My lifelines of the Word,
My guidance from the Holy Spirit within.
Sometimes the enemy uses my loved one.

Lord, You have not called me to battle giants.
My spiritual battle is to do
That which is my longing and delight:
To spend the time and effort to be close to You
Whom I love above life itself,
In order that I may have the strength and joy
To please my Lord, Whose I am.
There is no victory without You, Lord,
No hope or joy or peace outside Your Way.
Knowing the Truth, I can be free
If I have courage to live by that Truth.
In Christ Jesus I will conquer Satan's negatives.

14. Shadows

Mysterious shadows, uncertain their identity,
Dreaded in our ignorance, vanish in the light—
And yet it was the light that brought the shadows—
Of what? Never of nothing.
On one side of something, the light;
On the other, the shadow.

Shadows of Jesus, like Joseph and Joshua,
Moses and Melchesidec, David and Solomon:
Shadows of the Real cast back into time
By the Almighty God Who is Light

Are imperfect images, but proof that the real exists.
Yet when the Light has fully come,
Where are the shadows?
Memories, reminders of faith and hope.

The Law of Moses, with its somber negatives
And its proscriptions was a shadow
Of the perfect Law of Love
Revealed by Jesus on the cross.
Bathed in the Light of God's perfect love,
When the Real had come,
The shadows vanished, nailed to the cross,
To be seen only by those on the dark side of light.

We are in the Light and the Light is in us,
And we are the Light if He lives in us.
But sometimes our imperfections
Make shadows as we spread the Light.
God's promises, every one we claim and meet the ifs,
Are shadows of reality He has created just for us.
By faith we accept each promise as real,
Following in faith that shadow
Until the glorious reality is manifest
In the fullness of His Light.

Thank You, dear Father, for the dark side of Light,
The shadows we can follow
To the Reality in Your promises.

15. Imitation Prophecy

Satan has his prophets who outline his plans,
Often hidden in obscure volumes—
(Are they imitation bibles?)—
Or proclaimed from headlines.
Oh, yes, Satan has his plans for his eternal purpose:

To rule the world as god.
He knows his hidden plans are vain,
So like a spoiled brat, sometimes
He shifts them to destruction.
("If I can't have it, I'll ruin it
So no one else can have it.")
If he cannot be the Lord God Omnipotent,
He will be god of the damned,
And get as large a kingdom as he can.

Dictators, tyrants, sorcerers are his prophets.
Hitler did not hide his intentions,
But outlined them in "Mein Kampf,"
And broadcast them to the world.
He hid only that they were of Satan.
Communists do not hide their plans—
They're out for all the world to see,
In blatant prophecy,"We will bury you!"
But, blinding eyes, Satan
Like a snake, hypnotizes his victims.

The New Age Movement,
The religion of Satan's planned empire,
Is advertised in enticing colors,
And reasoned goals of world peace,
Ruled by the coming Antichrist.
He plans worldwide unity of worship.
That prophecy is published everywhere,
In newspapers, school books, TV,
Developed in false cults, secret societies,
In humanistic distortions of God's Word,
So cleverly that it deceives even God's elect
Unless they are wise in His Word.

But Satan's prophets fail the test:
That every prophecy must come to pass, every one.
The Jean Dixons and Edgar Caseys,
Nostradamuses, Hitlers and Lenins
Predict in ignorance Satan's hollow hopes,
While God's Word, forever settled in heaven,
Continues to come to pass.

16. In the Dark of Midnight

In the dark of midnight
I wander restless through the house,
Familiar with door and walls,
Looking for the light of dark—
Moonlight and streetlight through the windows,
Faint nightlight in the hall,
Red numbers of electric clocks,
Charge-light of razor and circuit breaker—
Everywhere tiny lights conquer the dark.

In the midnight of my soul
I wander through my life
Familiar with daily tasks,
Comfortable with loving friends,
But restless with tasks not done,
With longings not expressed,
With the intruding space
That keeps me separate from God—
No, never!
For I know He is here:
His Light sparkles in the dark,
In a golden leaf reflecting,
In sun-fire in the water,
A rainbow in dew,

A long-remembered melody,
A word of love, a touch,
His Word peaking out
From the hidden treasure in my heart—
Everywhere tiny lights
Conquer the dark.

17. Jesus Wept

Jesus looked over the world
He had died to save,
And saw so many who didn't know Him
And His mighty Word of love,
Who were suffering pain and sorrow,
Trapped in sin, and ignorance,
And He wept.

"Ye have not because ye seek not"—
Oh that ye would seek and receive."
Pray, my brothers, that our Father may do
His mighty works in each of us in need
In all the world,
That His perfect will be done.
Ask, and receive.
He waits—and weeps.

18. Strings

My Lord says, "Go ye into all the world
And preach the gospel to every creature."
Like a wild horse, I head for the gate,
Full of oats, on fire, eager—
And then the bridle of submission
Turns me into little circles within my corral,
Quiet, or neighing softly to receptive ears.

My Lord says,
"Bring all your tithes into the storehouse."
Reaching for the purse of his and mine,
I find the string pulled tight,
And tied against our tithe.
I lay upon the altar a tenth part
Of the pittance that is mine,
And humbly ask my Lord to show me
How to use the little rest for Him.
In Cadillac and furs, my heart feels poor.

My Lord says,
"Give and it shall be given unto you"—
I give my love, and God returns in overflowing measure;
I give my time, and God multiplies the minutes;
I give my talents, watch them grow,
And take seed in others,
Spreading joy that lights my life,
Uncovering hidden talents without end.
But the forbidding tape of submission
Keeps our treasures here on earth.

My Lord says, "Wives, submit yourselves
Unto your own husbands as unto the Lord."
And my Lord also says,
"And everyone that hath forsaken houses
Or brethren, or sisters, or father or mother,
Or wife or children, or lands, for my name's sake
Shall receive an hundredfold,
And shall inherit everlasting life."
And also, "If any man come to me
And hate not his father and mother,
And wife, and children, and brothers and sisters,
And his own life also, He cannot be my disciple."
No mention of husband.

Lord, I long to be Your disciple.
When I submit to my husband,
Why does my heart break
In ignoring forbidden commands?

19. Flesh, You Are Dead

Flesh, you are dead, crucified with Christ.
How dare you, like an unruly dog
Knock over trash cans looking for garbage,
Or gobble up crumbs, lick any stranger's hand,
Or sit up and beg for unhealthy dainties?
Does not your master provide plentiful and perfect food?
How dare you pull the leash with your master
Into mud or posted property?
Or break the leash to run uncontrolled?
Like a seeing-eye dog, be willing to be trained,
To sit and stay, lead and protect on command,
To wait in eager appreciation for his choice of food,
To answer love with love, and, for love, obey—
To be eyes and hands and feet in this world,
For only in Him do you have life today?
Body, be trained and obedient to serve your Master.

Flesh, you are dead, crucified with Christ.
You are a costume I wear
On the stage of the world,
Designed to promote the Author's purpose and theme,
Suitable for my God's assigned role
Of speaking the Gospel Words of my Playwright,
Obedient to my Holy Spirit Director.
Costumes don't direct the action, or steal the show.
They silently project character, accent dialogue.
Body, glorify the Author of your faith.

Flesh, you are dead, crucified with Christ.
You are a robot servant in a contaminated world,
With cleverly fashioned eyes, ears, tongue,
With well-designed hands and locomotion,
Created to carry the Word to the lost,
To demonstrate God's love and mercy to the poor,
Programmed and controlled
Through a Word-trained brain,
Receptive to stimuli of the needy,
But led and empowered by the Holy Spirit,
Committed to the will of the Almighty God.
Servants don't dally, decide, or demand.
They listen, follow and obey.
Body, delight to serve and obey your Eternal Master.

Flesh, you are dead, crucified with Christ.
Only in Him do you seem to live this moment
To be a temple, a costume, a servant,
His entry ticket into a rebelling world.
Body, be an abiding place for the Holy Spirit;
Be a costume through which the character of God is seen;
Be a servant that God's eternal will be done.
Flesh, you are dead, crucified with Christ.
But Life lives in you.

20. Heavy Sorrow

Last year, a heavy sorrow underlined your joy;
Last year a pinch of pain punctured your peace and
praise;
But you overcame doubts and fears
By your steadfast faith;
Last year's loneliness was the background
For the love that glows on your face.

Planted in rich soil of faith,
Watered with living water of love,
Surrounded by Life-giving Light,
May this year's praise-seed blossom
In bouquets of brightest joy.

For the One who loves us guards our years,
Designs the final art.
He gives the love, joy, peace and praise—
To yield in faith is our simple part.

21. No Time for Living

You say we have no time for living.
Have we misused our hours, our days?
We have been granted our full measure,
Free to allot in our chosen ways.

What is living? What tasks are part,
Well worth our time and attention?
And which are detours or wasted time,
Keeping our lives in detention?

You manage money beautifully,
Study to make decisions wise;
You keep house and yard in good repair,
Alert to adjust as our taxes rise.

Meals and dishes, making dirty clothes clean,
Occasional vacuum, sweep and dust,
Shop and sew, write letters, send gifts—
Sort papers if I really must—

Is this living? Doing what we need to do?
Or is living what we do when these things are through?
Is our living the news, watching things on TV?
Playing bridge with friends, time with family, too?

Should our God have a part of our living time?
Is the purpose of our lives His will?
Or is time spent with Him a hindrance
Stolen from time our "living" should fill?
Is real living the time we are sharing
Any place, any time, one on one?
Or may it be that that living begins
When our life on this earth is done?

God's Word tells me my eternal life
Began when I asked Jesus to be my Lord.
Any time that does not include Him is lost.
He's the Way, Truth, and Life—That's the Word.

Whether we have time for living or not,
Our lives on earth soon will be through.
Our life on earth is the time to do
Exactly what He's asked us to do.

22. Ifs and Thens

If we could just remember
All the ifs God outlined for us,
Then we could claim the promises,
With peace and joy, be prosperous.

But since we forget,
Trespass again and again,
God in His love has built a bridge
Over the "ifs" into the "thens".

And if we but ask,
Set around Him our goals,
He'll send a guide for the way,
Avoiding pitfalls and holes.

23. Sounding Brass, Tinkling Cymbals

Too late.
Days have slipped into weeks,
Weeks into months,
And they are gone.
Love and caring, flat,
Like opened, unused soda,
Useless now.
Like good intentions,
Love unexpressed,
Prayers without feet—
Worthless.

And all the hours of prayer,
All the Bible studies,
All the carbon copies typed,
All the self, shared on demand,
All the helpful errands,
All the hours of telephone-listening,
All the handwork and stitching,
Canned peaches and applesauce,
Church work and housework—
All not worth a friend.

Passive, I let routine
And telephones and scheduled events
Regulate my days and weeks and months.
They fill every moment I allow,
And leave me spent.

Routines and telephones and scheduled events
Take my love, freely offered.
I release, but do not send,
Relinquishing initiative,
Like a cow waiting to give milk.
Come, I say. Love should go.

Procrastinator:
Doing everything but what I knew
Is what I want to do.
Wormlike, I build a cocoon around myself
In my unscheduled time
With reading, sewing, anything
That can avoid the piles of papers,
Letters to answer, steps of love.
And then I see myself with contempt.
Hypocrite;
Teaching love, hiding from reality.
People ask me how, in my allotted time,
Twenty-four hours a day, seven days a week,
I can do so much. No wonder there:
I steal the time for doing of the Word
And spend it on secondary works.

Lord Jesus, I have been so busy
Sharing the wonder of You in Your Word
That I have missed You in the eyes of my friend,
That I have failed to visit You when You were sick,
That I have withheld the written word of love
To You across the miles.

Too late.
How can one ask forgiveness for the unforgivable?
How can one learn to do the Love
Day by day, right away?

False humility:
I would disturb my friend, I rationalize—
Too early in the morning, or she might be napping.
I ask, who am I that it matters;
Who would care whether I come or not.
Hypocrite!
Even if my presence does not matter to my friend,
It matters to me, and to You, Lord Jesus.
If I say You are in me,
Then not my love, but Yours is longed for,
And it makes a difference if I—and You—are there;
And if I am not there, am I saying that You do not care?
Blasphemy!

What is caring, Lord?
I pray for, I ask about, I think of those I love . . .
All intangible.
My heart aches for, longs for . . .
Really? How would one know?
Teach me, O Lord, to get my love
Out from the inside to the outside,
To make it real in the real world,
To be a doer of the Word, not a hearer only.
Too late.
Are there others, Lord,
Where it might not be too late?
Am I still teachable?
Or is it too late for me, too.
I want to begin again—
Lord, can one be born again again?
Make life simple again,
And teach me to love like You.
Lord, teach me to love like You.

24. Oh, That I Were Worthy!

When I consider the holiness of Thy Name,
So glibly called on in confidence,
Profaned by thoughtless sophisticates,
Disdained by arrogant atheists,
I weep.
O that I were worthy to call upon Thy Name!
When I consider the mercy in Thy Name,
Forgiving seven times seventy our stumblings,
Hating our sins, but loving us,
Despite willful ignorance, selfishness, greed,
Ever ready to receive repenting hearts,
Even unto providing the Way—
What grief for Thee to know
That such sacrifice alone could atone;
What pain for Thee to see
The sufferings of Your Son—
I weep.
Oh, that I were worthy of that suffering!

When I consider the love of the Lord,
Limitless, endless,
Surrounding, filling, overflowing
Even the least of these, His creatures,
Source of all love, man's highest goal,
Seeing beyond sin to anguished heart,
Caring even when rejected and despised,
Giving without demanding in return,
Yet multiplying any love we give to Thee,
Adding peace and joy,
I weep.
Oh, that I were worthy of Thy love!

When I consider the power of Thy Name,
Conferred on us who accept Thy new life,
Who humbly bear the Name of Christ, Thy Son,
And as His body serve Thy holy will,
Scarcely claiming half the promises,
Hardly wielding half the power,
Scarcely divining half Thy purpose,
Like babies presuming on Thy patience,
Waiting through gentle suggestions
For the harsher command,
Resenting denials and corrections,
Rushing to serve you in our own way
—Yet even so, empowered in that Name—
I weep.
Oh, that I were worthy of that Power.

When I consider the wisdom of Thy Word,
Preserved in inspired writings,
Waiting to be ingested in our hearts,
Interpreted by Thine indwelling Spirit,
Released in power through our lips
But so often lightly scanned and sorted,
Superficially honored in infrequent snatches,
Analyzed, criticized, dissected by our scholars,
Rejected by scornful intellectuals and ignorant fools,
Yet even so, so wise and powerful
That not one Word returns to Thee empty,
I weep.
Oh that I were worthy of Thy Word.

When I consider the gift of Thy Holy Spirit,
Deigning to dwell in this imperfect temple,
To teach and guide and purify,
To use as instrument,
I weep.
Oh, that I were worthy to be Thy temple!

When I consider my old, unworthy self
Shed like an empty cocoon, dead,
And when to my reborn spirit,
Eternally alive in Him,
Christ adds His Holy Spirit—
Does His Infinite Spirit added even to nothing,
Not make that nothing infinite?
But I am forgiven, washed clean,
Clothed in His righteousness,
Empowered with His Name!
How can my worthiness be measured?
Hallelujah! In His eyes, I am worthy!

25. Slow Learners

Why, Oh Lord,
Does our little church swirl in quiet eddies,
Instead of rushing in torrents of Living Water?
Why do we hold up our smoking lamp
Instead of turning the switch
To flood the world with the bright glory of our Lord?
Why do we peddle along with aching legs on our tricycle
While the 10-speed power of the Spirit
Races past us on every side?

Why do we set our pace by the slowest in our midst,
Rather than holding their hands and racing all together
As fast as the Holy Spirit leads?
And if some drag their feet,
Lift them with loving hands;
And if they reject Your Spirit even then,
Let go, and keep up with God.

Why do we hear and read Your Word
In little, soon-forgotten sections
Instead of plunging deep into its wonder
And meditating on it day and night?
Why do we seek the Holy Spirit on our own terms,
Rejecting some gifts,
Asking portions (not too much) of others,
Preferring known cupfuls
To waves of light and power?
Why is our big sanctuary half full
While little homes or big convention halls
Overflow with eager seekers?

Lord, is Your church divided into tracts,
For slow-learners, born-agains,
And hungry spirits tirelessly, enthusiastically
Seeking Thy truth in Thy Word, in prayer,
In the depths of their spirit
Communing with the Holy Spirit within?
Do we slow-learners even dream
Of the glories awaiting our asking?

Oh, Lord God Omnipotent,
I see Your power today sweeping nations,
Filling hundreds, thousands, millions
With Your Holy Spirit,
Working miracles in healing, in open doors,
In perfect timing for outreach overseas,
In taking Your Word in power by printed book,
By airways, by video tape, satellite,
Behind bamboo, iron and voodoo curtains,
Into islands, jungles and ghettos,
Into prisons, Satan's own bodyguard,
Even into hearts media-conditioned,
Complacent in their religions.

Why not, Oh Lord,
Come into our church with power,
Melting our hearts into one,
So that we yield to Your Son as Savior and Lord,
Overflowing love to one another and others,
Pouring the Holy Spirit into us?
Do we not pray enough? Have faith enough?
(We have our measure, Lord.)
Are we not totally committed?
Are our spirits not yielded?
Or is it just that it is not yet
The fullness of Your time?

But Lord, put that yearning for You in our hearts.
When Your Holy Spirit fills our hearts,
Can we help praying, believing, feeding, loving?
Will we not yearn to do Your will?
Come, Oh Lord, in Your fullness,
And move our church into the mainstream of Your will.

26. Roar!

Roar!
Get angry!
Shake your fist at God!
So He didn't heal you.
Well, you didn't expect Him to, did you?
What claim do you have on Him?
Love? He's not your Father yet.

So He didn't take care of your debts.
Were you faithful with the money you had?
Were you a good steward?
Did you give God His tenth?
Have you laid up treasures in heaven
For Him to draw for you in your need?

Oh, you don't believe in God,
Not in a loving God Who cares, anyway.
He hasn't treated you as if He cares,
And you prayed, too . . . sort of.
Went to church, too,
Pretty regularly for a while.
Wasted all that time and effort.
You even read the Bible. Through.
He's muffed His chances with you, hasn't He?
So there!

Who does God think He is, anyway,
Telling you that you have to come to Him
His Way, or not at all?
You're not a sinner;
Well, you're not all that bad,
Better than most.
Never hurt anyone, never stole, never murdered,
Honored your parents, never stayed angry long.
Repent? Of what? Why should you?
What if this man—Son of God, they say—
Died for you?
You didn't ask Him to.

And that business about Lord!
Ask Christ to be Savior and Lord,
Lord of your whole life!
Commit yourself completely to Him?
No way! You have your pride.
And you're going to get through this on your own.

Roar!
Get angry!
Shake your fist at God!
Challenge Him!

Say, all right, God,
If You exist, show me,
But make it worth His while,
Be willing to be shown,
And when you see that God is real,
Give in. Obey. Follow.
Say, "God, convince me, and I'm Yours."
But you have to ask to be His,
Yield your all for His all,
All or nothing.
It's your choice: for Him or against Him;
Life—or death.
Double-mindedness gets you nothing.
Luke-warmness gets you spewed out of His mouth.
Almost persuaded is lost.

What is faith?
Is it real?
Faith is the substance (That's something real. Heb. 11:1)
Of things hoped for,
The evidence (that's proof) of things not seen.
Faith is the proof of itself, the reality of itself.
Where do you find faith if you have none?
Or not much?
It doesn't grow on trees, you know.
Faith comes from hearing the Word of God.
(Really listening, really hearing.)
Ask God to help you hear.
There's only one Way, Jesus Christ.
"For God so loved the world (you)
That He sent His only begotten Son
That whosoever (that's you) believeth on Him
Might be saved." (John 3:16)
Believe. Be saved. Have everlasting life.

But what if, after you have made this big commitment,
Given the all that you are, all that you have—
The suffering and pain,
Problems and poverty,
Frustration and resentment,
Doubt and fear,
Hope and love—
After you have given all this in faith to Him,
As far as you can see, your faith is left fruitless?
You are holding the same suffering and pain,
Problems and poverty, frustration and resentment,
Doubts and fears, hopes and love—
What have you gained?
What have you lost?

You've lost eternal damnation;
You've lost the aloneness of carrying your burdens—
"Cast all your burdens upon the Lord,
And He will sustain you."
You've exchanged your burdens
For Christ's yoke (which is light).
You've gained the right to eternal life in Christ.
You've gained each of His more than 500 promises,
Including healing and prosperity,
As your faith grows to appropriate them.
You've gained a purpose, the Great Commission.
You've joined the winning team.
You gain the potential of producing fruit
Like Love, Peace, Joy, Self-control,
Patience, Godliness, Faith, Gentleness,
Meekness, and of receiving spiritual gifts.
You've gained a heavenly Father Who loves you
With a greater love than you can dream of;

A Brother and Lord in Christ
Who promises never to leave you;
And a Comforter and Teacher
Who comes to live within you.
And more—there's always more—
You lose the world,
And gain the Pearl of Great Price
Which lasts forever.

Roar! Get angry!
Shake your fist at God!
Deny that He is!
Will that make Him disappear?
Will that take away the pain?
Go ahead, Roar!

27. Being Set Free

(Meditation on John 8:31-32: "Then said Jesus to those Jews which believed on Him, 'If ye continue in my word, then are ye my disciples indeed; and ye shall know the truth, and the truth shall make you free.'"

Lord, where have I gone astray?
Your Word have I loved,
And to meditate on Your Word is my delight.
In my heart do I hide it,
And it is continually on my lips.
I know Your Word is truth,
That You and Your Word are one.
I know the power of your Word as seed, or sword,
In creation, growth, fulfillment,
Warfare, protection, healing . . .
I am in awe of the beauty and power
Of Your precious, everlasting Word of Truth.

Why do I not feel free?
Am I really free, but trapped
By outlaw thoughts and feelings?
Why do I, like a dog on a leash,
Strain against restraint,
Limited to controlled, permitted freedom?
Is there really a leash?
Or do I myself contain both the pull and the restraint?
Are You, dear Lord, the leash, holding me back
Through my husband's unspoken disapproval?
Or are You longing to have me break away,
To plunge without a restraint into the heady joy
Of learning the Word, hearing testimonies,
Serving, teaching?

Dear Lord, how can I please both You and him?
He thinks the Word, the fellowship and faith
Are foolishness.
How can I please You, dear Lord,
If I rebel against my husband?
Is being a homemaker and wife
All You ask of me? I think not.

In my heart You have put this fire for Your Word;
You have anointed me to teach that Word.
I have tasted the fullness of joy in Your presence,
The oneness with You and Yours
In the fellowship of praise and worship.
Lord, I want to abandon myself in You,
To live and breathe and have my being in You,
To share Your wonderful Word with others.
That's the freedom I yearn for.
But selfishly, perhaps, dear Lord,
I want my husband at my side
Serving You, abiding in Your Word,
Submerged with me in the joy of Your presence.

If I have to choose, there is no choice—
It's You, Lord, all the way.
There is no other way.
You assure me that no matter where I go,
No matter what I do or how I serve,
You are in control of my life,
Unless, in foolishness, I rebel,
And try to guide my life myself.

Lord, give me the wisdom
To know which restraints are from You,
And see those as Your gentle care,
And which are of my carnal self, or the world,
Or my husband's worldly will.
And with prayer and faith loose myself
Of any restraints that are not of You.
Sometimes, dear Lord, it isn't so simple to see.
Help me to focus on Your will, Your Word, Your voice,
And rest in You.

28. Sometimes I Want to Soar

Oh, Lord, sometimes I want to soar—
Strengthened by Your Word,
Mounting on wings of prayer,
Pull up, up, up into the limitless sky
And soar free in Your limitless air,
Lifted by Holy Spirit winds,
Resting on You Who are there.

Sometimes I want to dig deep
Searching for treasures in Your Word,
Meditating in fertile soil, growing roots
Out to the living water,
Down to the rock of commitment,
And wait patiently for sprout, bloom and fruit.

Sometimes I want to share Your Word.
It is too big to hold inside,
Too wonderful in its simplicity,
The forever of It suddenly too new,
The parallel truths of It, Old and New,
Revealed as one in the infinity twist,
Like a Noebus strip,
The infinite eternity of you on each page
Overflowing in loving kindness,
Reaching out to draw us to You.
All eternity cannot exhaust the richness of Your Word.

Sometimes I want to shout
In the wonder of Your Word,
To sing and dance in exuberant joy,
In awe of Your majesty and power,
Of the everlasting mercy and love You employ.

Sometimes I need to share
The bounteous supplies in Your Word,
Knowing there are gifts of Your love, peace and wonder
Full enough to overflow every soul on earth.

But sometimes I want to cry
In despair of obedience to Your Word,
So short of Your expectations—and mine.
But You love me still, knowing all of me,
Forgive me, teach me, and I find
You accept me, Your child: You soothe my fears.
The wonder of it, the joy and hope of it
Leads to the release of happy tears.

Sometimes I want to run—
So powerful is Your living Word—
From, out of, to, into—Where? Why?
Does the struggle seem too hard?

Or too easy here in my comfort?
Is it easier to run than wait?
Or is it really Your call I've heard?

Sometimes I want to wait too long
For the absolute assurance of Your Word,
Concerned with stepping out on my own will or reason
Or abiding in dead deeds,
Or with following the Logos rather than the Rhema,
Forgetting that the Holy Spirit within will guide,
Forgetting that only a moving ship
Will follow the rudder's way.
But, oh, dear Lord, may the helm
Be in Your hands each day.

Sometimes I want to fight
When men ignore the power of Your Word,
When Your compassion calls me to set men free,
Or Your Love bids me join a brother's fight,
Or when weakness or temptation shows me my enemy.
Help me carefully put on Your armor,
Keeping it ready every day,
Polish the sword of Your Word by knowing Your Way.

Sometimes all I can do is stand,
In Your promises, strength, and love, rest and abide,
Knowing Who You are and Whose I am,
Trusting, enduring, rejoicing, praising,
Quietly listening for Your voice inside.
Oh Lord, sometimes I want to hide,
So great is my weakness revealed in Your Word,
Ashamed, rebellious, aware of my sin,
Too full of self to let You in,
And glad, deep inside, that You are there
To be my strength and share my joy.

Lord, sometimes I want to lose myself in You,
In praise and prayer, just worship and adore,
Absorbed in the glory of Your presence,
Receiving as much as I can hold—
And always longing for more.

Chapter V

You Give Me Glimpses of Yourself

1. More

There's always more;
You always offer more,
Never limited, always more.

When first we open our hearts
Just the tiniest crack,
You pour through that brokenness
The healing balm of Your love.
When we open the doors of our hearts,
You come in, as far as our opening permits,
Always waiting to be invited,
Never usurping more than we are ready to yield,
But always bearing gifts,
As many as we are ready to accept.

And when we yield the all to You,
What bounty You pour in!
You teach our hearts to grow,
To receive more and more,
To overflow.

And never in a lifetime—
In an eternity—
Can any man grow enough
To hold the all
That You are ready to give,
To overflow in rivers of Living Water
The fullness of Your love,
To shout far enough the Good News,
To understand and proclaim the half
Of the wonderful Truth of Your majesty
And power and Judgment and Mercy,
The holiness and Power of Your Name.

No matter how much we learn,
No matter how graciously we are filled,
No matter how selflessly we serve,
There is always more,
Infinitely more.

2. Who Can Number?

Who can number
        The grains of sand,
        Or the stars in the sky?
                                Not I.
And yet they have a number,
        A finite number
        With a limit
                                In it.
Only our Creator God
        Can number these, if He please,
        And wipe away a trillion or two,
                                Or make all new,
                                Or add a few.

Yet in Him, the infinite I
        In the infinite me can see,
        And enter into God's infinity,
                        Eternally one
                        With His Son.

3. Man of the Year

Ponder the qualifications:
Compare Him with the best,
Measure His accomplishments,
Submit Him to every test.

In Physics, He's Creator of Light and all things,
In Chemistry, changing water to wine,
In Medicine, healer of all who ask,
In Astronomy, planner of the measure of time.

Master carpenter, builder of the church eternal,
Engineer—designer of systems that rule;
Biologist who invented reproduction in kind,
Plus circulation, digestion, inner warmth and cool.

Meteorology—storms and rain obey His command;
Water cycle and winds purify and provide.
His Light is the source of all energy,
Through the sun, and all sources that in the earth hide.

All History centers on the day of His birth;
Wars are fought around His command.
His Word is the model of literary worth,
And the essence of all Life and Truth demand.

Philosophy, psychiatry, psychology, all
Are inferior to His wisdom of man's soul.
Compassion, philanthropy, all kinds of love—
Only He knows how to make man whole.

Find another, or a pair, or a group
In any field under the sun
That can challenge this Man
In His Work, in progress, or done.

Born nearly two thousand years ago,
But still alive and active, now and here,
He can lead any man or the whole human race.
I nominate Jesus for Man of the Year.

4. He Is Alive

He is alive!
He died, was buried,
Sealed and guarded in a tomb,
But He's alive, risen from the dead,
Alive forevermore.

Great men cast shadows through the years,
Their ideas linger, changing lives,
Inspiring hope, warning with fears,
But they are dead.
Abraham is dead, and David, too.
Ghengis Kahn and Caesar,
Alexander and Socrates,
Confucius, Bhudda, and Mohammed, dead.
Galileo and Rembrant,
Napoleon and Hitler,
Mao and Stalin, all dead.

They live in history and literature,
Until time, politics, or philosophy
Reduce the memories.
But Jesus is alive forevermore,
With us, in us, and we in Him.
He is Lord over all things on the earth,
Under the earth, and in heaven.
As God, he sits at the right hand
Of Almighty God, the Father,
And intercedes for us, His own,
Ready to return to judge the wicked,
And rule the world in righteousness.

But even now, as He reigns in heaven,
He is alive and present here on earth,
Not only in His reborn people,
But in His Word, His indwelling Holy Spirit,
His presence in our hearts, the Power of His name,
His power in His people, His overwhelming love.

He is alive!
He died, a horrible, painful death,
Was buried, sealed and guarded in a tomb,
But Death and Hell could not keep Him.
He arose and proved His life to many
Before He arose through the clouds to heaven.
He is alive.
The Lord and Savior of the world
Is alive forevermore.

5. Power Converter

Power—useful, dangerous,
Two twenty volts available through wire—
But for a 110 computer,
It's deadly.
Yet with a converter,
Useful power flows.

Power—unlimited, omnipotent:
Earthquake, tornado, plague—
These are deadly power.
But with the converter of faith,
This awesome power is on our side,
Accomplishing miracles,
Bringing joy and peace.

6. Humility

How can You, God, All-powerful Creator,
Perfect, righteous, omnipotent, omniscient,
Life, Light, Love, Upholder of all things,
Be humble?
And yet You love and forgive
The stumbler, the sinner, the scoffer, blasphemer,
And your church,
Not once, but seventy times seven times.

As Jesus, Your beloved Son,
You became a helpless baby,
A humble peasant carpenter,
A servant, who gave of Himself without stint,
Abundantly, even unto dying for us,
Suffering in Hell the penalty for our sins.
He remembered in His resurrection
To bring us, too, consenting to share
With us His inheritance as joint heirs.

He agreed to be the head of a stumbling church,
—yet a triumphant church—and intercedes
For each of us individually, and as His Church.
He even promises to honor this Church, Your Church,
As His bride for all eternity.

As Holy Spirit, Lord God Almighty,
How beautifully You reveal true humility.
You inspired prophets and kings
To be the channel for Your power and Word to earth,
But never do You intrude uninvited.
In Jesus You were the Godhead
He put aside to become man,
So that as man He might show us—
Might be—the Way
By living sinless in a sinful world.
Your living in Jesus to strengthen and guide
Shows Your wisdom and power,
But when You, Spirit of the living God,
Come to live in us, weak, babies in faith,
To teach, guide, empower us,
How humble You are!
And when we ask, You speak and pray through us.
What wonderful gifts You give us!
Yet You never speak of Yourself,
But always of Jesus, the Word,
Helping us understand and live that Word.
How humble You are!

Dear Father, Dear Lord Jesus, Dear Holy Spirit,
You have blessed us with innumerable gifts,
With countless promises, overflowing blessings.
May we give You joy by receiving
With confidence, with thankfulness,
With praises, with love, with serving,

But may we ever be humble,
Remembering the Source,
Remembering Whose we are,
Remembering that without You,
We are nothing.

7. When God Weeps

Who will comfort God when He weeps?
What? You do not think God weeps?

When Lucifer, His glorious archangel rebelled,
Did He not weep?
When Eve and Adam fell in disobedience,
Did He not weep?
And when Cain killed Abel?

When He had to send Moses
Interrupting their togetherness,
And the giving of the law and Truth,
To stop the worship of the golden calf,
Did He not weep?
When Jerusalem was so filled with apostasy,
Even idolatry, that He had to remove His Spirit,
Perhaps then He wept.
When God had to turn His face from His Son,
His beloved, only begotten Son,
And place the sin of all the world on Him,
And know that He would die and go to hell,
(Even though He also knew
That He would rise triumphant)
Surely He wept.

When His loved, adopted children were martyred
In the arenas of Rome, the Spanish inquisition,
His people herded into Nazi gas chambers,
Christians imprisoned and tortured in the Gulag;
When famines, floods, and plagues kill,
Wars and riots maim, destroy innocents and guilty,
How could He not weep?

And when His own church, the Body of Christ,
Grows luke-warm, is entangled in cults,
Even denies His name and His resurrection,
(Although He knows there is a godly remnant)
Is that not cause for God to weep?
And when He judges at the great white throne,
Those not written in the Book of Life,
Will He rejoice as he condemns to Hell?
Or will He weep?

Who will comfort God when He weeps?
Redeemed ones, praise Him and worship!
Bless His holy Name.
Love Him, honor Him, obey Him all the Way;
Rejoice in Him, and win souls for Him.
As His children, comfort Him.

8. There He Was

There He was—a sweet, helpless baby,
Born in a manger, just as God had planned
In promise and prophecy,
His fulfilled prophecy: the Word made flesh,
God's Gift to His beloved man,
His love, His hope, His eternal plan
Released into His sin-filled world.

What faith our Father God revealed
To place His one redemption plan
In the hands of a tiny baby boy!

There He was—
Thirty years without sin,
Suddenly Spirit-filled, led by the Holy Spirit,
Resisting and overcoming temptation,
Speaking only God's Word as He heard,
Doing only God's will as He saw Him doing,
The very image of His Father God,
Jesus Christ, the Messiah, the anointed One,
Loving, teaching, healing,
Revealing the Way of redemption for fallen man.
There He was—back torn by whips,
Head bleeding from thorns,
Nailed to a cross—
All for the sins of the world
Placed on Him, the Son of Man,
Our sinless Savior, forgiving,
Dying for me, for you, for all mankind.
Our penalty for sin He paid in full.

There He is—alive, risen from the dead,
Seated at God's right hand,
All man, all God,
Interceding for us.
Our mediator between God and man.

Here He is,
Always with us and in us,
As we live and serve in Him,
Protected taught, loved,
Safe for all eternity.

And there He will be—
Coming back to earth as He rose,
But now the King of Kings,
Lord of Lords.
Hallelujah!

9. Viewfinder

If a camera could imitate
The eyes of the Lord God Omnipotent,
It could focus on infinity
And sub-atomic particles,
And every star or tree in between—
Simultaneously.

Its universe-wide lens
Could present horizon to horizon,
With every detail included,
Undistorted.
It could adjust to any light—
Or lack of light—
(It would be the Light)
Infrared, xray, radiation,
Sun or searchlight,
All adequate, all together.

It could focus in depth,
Beneath the surface,
Inside the shell,
Behind the wall,
Unhampered.

It could adjust the time
To instant, or time-exposure
For any time, past or future,
Or bypassing time,
Give infinite exposure,
In eternity-lapse sequence.
It could capture motion
With no pause between frames,
From every angle.
It could compute not only distance and light,
But relationships and influences,
Causes and effects,
Among all things in all time,
And store all this data for eternity
With instant recall.

But if a camera could imitate
The eyes of the Lord God Almighty,
It would filter these views with love,
Coloring the actions with the desires of the heart,
The willingness to obey.
It would focus through the blood of Jesus
And photograph sparkling white,
The redeemed ones clothed in His righteousness,
The faltering life finished in Christ's perfection.

It would penetrate illusions,
Hypocrisy, cover-ups, self-deceptions,
To preserve Truth.

Oh, Lord,
Let me view Thy world, Thy universe,
Through Thy wondrous eyes,
And, Lord, see my open heart
With love-filtered, rose-colored glasses.

10. Armfuls of Treasures

God has armfuls of treasures He wants to give us.
Let's open our hearts to receive.
He's our Father Who loves us
More than we can imagine.
He knows the way through the wicked world,
And longs for us to take His hand,
To let Him guide us through the mine fields.
He knows where the joy is,
And longs to show us the sparkles and rainbows,
The quiet warmth of His presence,
The ecstasy of sharing with Him
In the depths of our souls
Until we merge into glorious oneness with Him,
Our Creator, our infinite and eternal God,
And in that oneness, He shows us His glory.
He has wisdom to share, and longs for us to ask.
He has a hungry love to pour on His children
So that through them He can show His love
To every hurting soul, and draw each one
Into His infinite heart.

He longs for us to share with Him
Our deepest secrets—although He knows them all—
So that He can fulfill our hearts desires,
Take away every stumbling block and heartache,
And fill us with everything we need
To conquer every enemy inside.
He's the Father Who loves us so much
That as Jesus, He died to set us free
To be His children. Forever.

11. Not Broadminded

God is not broadminded when it comes to other gods.
He tells us He alone is God; there are no others.
Does the Creator tell men to ignore Him,
And worship His creation?
Should men worship the sun, the moon, or stars
Which move passively in their Creator's ordered plan?
They have no power or wisdom
Apart from their Creator.

What of idols?
God tells us what He thinks of them:
Man-made, dumb, helpless, powerless things.

Man-made philosophies are ignorance
Searching for the Truth, and missing the mark.
They wear their garments of wisdom,
But also blinders to the Word of Truth
Which God reveals to all who will to see.

Great men with great ideas are admirable—
Confucius, Buddha, Aristotle, Mohammed—
They cast shadows beyond their times,
But they are dead;
Their ideas are but glimpses of the Truth.
Why worship a dead man whose sliver of truth
Is shaped into a philosophy and way of life,
But has no doorway into Eternity?

In arrogant pride, man invents his gods,
Unwilling to accept his lack of omniscience,
And tries to rule with his illusion of omnipotence.
But where is Jesus?
How sad to invent the false
When the Real is available
Through humility and prayer!

In all His universe, God reveals Himself:
All science is unveiling the wonders
God had long ago created.
God reaches out to His beloved man,
Trying to lure Him into Faith with loving care
And eternal Words of Truth to guide his way.
He even sent His Son to save, and lead the Way,
The only Way to eternal life with Him.
When God has made His Way so clear in His Word,
Why do men seek other gods and other ways?
There is no other Way.

12. Hear Our Prayers, O gods

As conflicts rage and children die
All over the world,
Each of us prays to his god.
Muslims pray to Allah to help them conquer the Serbs,
To win back Cashmere,
Or push Israel out of "their" Palestine.
While multiplying Christians in China and Cuba
Pray for protection against Communists,
Muslims ask Allah to exterminate Christians.
In most of Africa, tribes pray to their gods,
To spirits, nature, Muslims to Allah, Christians to God,
Each asking victory over the others.
Hindus and Buddhists pray to their gods
Sometimes merely for the next meal,
While some offer their first born to the River god.
Could it be that all of them are praying
To the same one true God?
How can gods answer such conflicting prayers?

Let the gods call a convocation:
Let them meet together
To find agreement on what is right,
Set boundaries for authority to lessen conflict,
And then may the gods keep their agreements.

But if all the gods are One,
Why all the conflicts?
Who dares to oppose the One Most High God?
Stubborn men and their misguided lusts or greed?
Or is there one behind all the conflicts
Who hates the One Most High God?
Does he in his rage stir up hatred in men and nations?
Does he create false gods for them to worship
And laugh at their futility?
Does he gloat at opposition to the God he hates?

God is not divided, nor does He promote conflict.
Our God is One, a God of love for all
To care for, provide for all who are His own.
Satan's lesser, imitation gods will fall,
And Satan will be forever defeated.
God's peace will then spread all over all.

13. Why Is God Good?

Why is God good?
Is it because He is the Creator
And sets the standards of right and wrong,
Of good and bad, of pleasing Him and angering Him?
Do we define our terms as dictated
By the wishes and whims of our Creator?

What if by some fate more tragic than nightmares
Baal were indeed the creator and ruler?
Would we think it good to sacrifice our children?
To celebrate creation with official prostitution?
Would we live in fear of a capricious being
Who meted out rain and sun in return for sacrifice,
And pouted and withheld favor if we goofed?

What if Lucifer had not failed,
And he were now seated on God's throne,
Ruler not only of the world in measured moments
But of the heavens as well?
What would be our good to please
A Lucifer enthroned as god?
Would what we now regard as evil,
Actions inspired by Satan's bitterness—
Self-interest, deceit, hate, violence—
Really please Satan if he were god?

Or Pan—what kind of good would Pan require
If he were god—or would he care?
Would pandemonium be the rule?
And doing what comes naturally?
Would we have no aspirations of higher good?
Would there even be any spiritual side?
Would we be mere animals with better brains?

How could man measure good if there were no god?
Would some evolving sense of general welfare
Be the measure of our right and wrong?
With laws the substitute for conscience
And ethics the determiner of morality?
What is best for mankind (who decides what is best?)
Would be the goal.

How gratefully I worship God, my Creator,
And strive to grow into His goodness,
So glad there is so kind a standard,
So loving a Guide, so merciful a Judge.
It is my Father's world, and I like it that way.

14. Before the Beginning (John 1:1-2; Genesis 1:1-3)

In the beginning was—What? Who?
Before the beginning was—was, existed,
Before anything was created,
Before there was any time,
God was. He existed.
He is the very essence of existence;
He is what existence is;
He is Life, what Life is.

But in the beginning
Was the Word.
And the Word was with God,
And the Word was God.
The Word—the expression of ideas,
Exchange of thoughts in words,
Between God—?
And the Word Who was God?

And in the beginning was the Spirit,
Hovering, brooding over the waters,
Waiting in the darkness for the Word.

Before the beginning,
In the always of eternity,
In the limitlessness of infinity,
The Essence of Life, which is God,
Discussed ideas and plans,

Shared love with His inner being—
The Holy Spirit of the Holy God—
And with the Word Who is God,
Put his ideas and thoughts
Into reality that could be shared.

Part of the very essence of God
Is His Word, the expression of His creative thoughts
Which are real, eternal, powerful.
God is one, in three persons,
And the three Who are always one
Bring their innermost thoughts,
Ideas, longings, plans into existence
With the eternal Word.
When released, each ever-existent Word
Echoes forever throughout eternity,
And expands beyond
The endless edges of infinity.
In created Time and Space:
God selectively preserved
In His written Word,
And enshrined in human flesh
His Holy Word
To be the eternal Savior of Mankind.

Tremble, oh man, with the awesome reality
That the infinite Holy Spirit dwells in you,
And that your recreated spirit feeds and grows
By absorbing, "eating"
The eternal, powerful Word of God, who is God,
So that you who believe
And follow His commandments
Grow into the very image of God, your Creator,
Who created you to spend eternity with Him.

Thank Him Praise Him,
Grow by absorbing His Word,
And serve Him in the power
Of His indwelling Holy Spirit.

15. A Matter of Grammar

When Jehovah, Who is Salvation, Lord of all infinity,
Introduces Himself, He uses nouns, His Names:
"I am the Lord your God, the God of Abraham;"
I am your Provider, your Banner, your Peace,
Your Healer, your Shepherd, your Sanctifier."

When Jesus our God walked the earth as man,
In nouns He revealed His divine nature, His names:
"I am the Way, the Truth, and the Life . . .
"The Light of the World, Living Water,
'The Living Word, Bread of Life, the Good Shepherd,
"Your Righteousness"—all nouns.
God is, Jesus is what His name is.

We sidestep the mysterious identity with adjectives:
"God is so good," "Wonderful," "Marvelous,"
He is righteous, omnipotent, omniscient.
Oh, and yes, He is all of these, and more,
But we avoid the Names, the essence of our God.
There's power in the Name of Jesus.
God is His Name. Salvation—that is Jesus.
He is our Shepherd, Righteousness, Healer, Peace,
Our Sanctifier, Provider, our Lord and our God.

Like the 58 facets of the diamond,
Each picturing the heart,
His Names reveal the infinite facets of our God.
He is to us whatever we can believe He is
According to the revelation of His Word.

And when the eternal God moves in time,
His Names, those nouns, change to powerful verbs:
Love loves, Light lights, enlightens,
Life enlivens, Provider provides, Healer heals—
God in action in time and space.
Think of God as nouns,
The power of His infinite Names,
And in verbs, those Names in action in time and space.
And as we become like Him, noun by noun,
Let us move in His Nature, in His Power,
Verb by verb.

16. The Gemstone

Buried deep in the earth in mud,
Rough, shapeless rock,
Worthless to unpracticed eye,
But hard, hard, and ready to reflect
From some scraped edge any glimmer of light.
Rescued from the deep mud,
Washed, and bought with a price,
With what deep caring it is examined by the Master
For flaws and cleavage.
He weighs and tests it for hidden values,
Divides it in imagination many ways
Into most valued jewel,
Or relegated to serviceable drills and chips,
With even the dust treasured.

Only after dreams and plans, and skilled evaluation
Does the Master strike the crucial blow
To break along invisible planes
According to the Creator's design,
For the perfect jewel, fifty-eight times broken.
Then He polishes—no lesser substance can polish—
First rough, then oh, so gently,
Each surface in turn, to perfect smoothness.

Then the light, that wonderful Light,
Reflects from whichever facet is turned to receive;
Or, wonder of wonders,
The gemstone absorbs the Light
Into its crystal-clear flawlessness.
The Master's treasure flashes rainbow colors
To glorify the Light in perfect selflessness.

How can we measure value
But in the glory of the Creator
Recognized, revealed, reflected?

17. Omnipotence

Power, all power, omnipotence—
How can we imagine limitless power?
He created the heavens and the earth.
He said, "Light be!" and Light was.
Not only did the Lord God Almighty
Create the stars, sun, and moon,
But He started them spinning on their axes,
Swirled them into precise, controlled orbits,
Counterbalanced by gravity—Power,
Limitless, controlled power.

He made all degrees of power—
How could man dream
Of power compacted into an atom?
Of multiplied atoms releasing
Controlled power to conquer space?
Of invisible sun rays lifting invisible water
To hurl it down in hail,
Or gently let it drift to earth in snow,
Or by gravity pull it drop by drop
To wear a canyon in a plateau?
Or of seeds multiplying and breaking rocks?

He engineered perfect systems, complex, consistent.
Like water cycles, jet streams,
Atomic tables, chemical formulas,
Waves of light and heat—ultra violet to infra red—
Analyzing substances, measuring distances,
The cosmic yardstick of the speed of Light.
He devised action and reaction, leverage,
Patterns in and primes of numbers,
The law of Genesis, like reproducing like,
Seedtime and harvest, DNA,
The law of sin and death and life,
The interdependence of photosynthesis
Symbiosis, families and societies.
He invented economics, compounding, innovation,
(Even in God's kingdom)
And the wonder of the physical systems in man
Such as digestive, nervous, muscular, circulation,
All controlled, self-repairing, working in power.

He restrains His omnipotence!
I marvel at God's patience and restraint.
He chooses to give us power
Even to resist His will,
To rebel even against His omnipotence,
Or to destroy ourselves and others,
Relying only on the power of His love and righteousness
To draw us into His plan of grace.

He shares His omnipotence!
Yes, God shares His power with us
When we choose to follow Him.
He permits us to use His all powerful Name,
His Word with His power coiled within,
Ready to be released when we speak it in faith
To accomplish that for which He sent it.

He sent Himself in His Holy Spirit to live in us,
And release His omnipotence to work His will
Through our obedience and yieldedness.

Lord God Omnipotent,
How can we imagine Your limitless power?

18. Incredible, Impossible!

That there was Time and Space
(Where did they come from?)
And matter in an incredibly big mass
(Where did matter come from?)
That exploded in a big bang—
Incredible, impossible!

That this exploding matter by accident
Expanded into expanding groups
Into galaxies, stars, and black holes,
Made up of identifiable elements,
Each with its source of energy,
Organized in mathematical tables,
Moving in organized, predictable patterns—
Incredible, impossible!

That systems and laws of physics developed,
Predictable, identifiable:
Gravity gathering into systems,
Axis tilt arranging seasons, heat and cold,
Light and dark, consistent, in patterns;
Weather systems, solar systems,
Chemical, physical, ecological systems,
(No one planned and organized them?)
Incredible, Impossible!

And where did Life come from?
Virus, amoebae, seaweed and fish,
Each with its own DNA,
Reproducing only its own kind,
Predictable, identifiable (By accident?)
Incredible, Impossible!

And through eons of evolution, by chance,
A creature with a mind that could understand
All this accidental diversity,
Catalog, dissect, even rearrange
Atoms and DNA, explain evolution,
Develop and use forms of power.
One that could communicate, create, think,
(All this developed by chance)
Incredible, impossible!

And yet, could there be a God,
An intellect, a power, a wisdom
So immense that it could create
All this time and space and matter,
All this diversity, and even life itself?
(Where could this Creator come from?)
Incredible, impossible!

Before He began creating Time and Space,
Did He plan all this diversity?
All these systems, predictable,
Coordinated, reproducible?
And where did Life come from?
How could He create a man
Who could discover, catalog and wonder
At His diverse creation,
And even communicate with His Creator?
Incredible, impossible!

How do we choose an explanation
Of the incredible and impossible?
Do we believe in the incredible accidents,
Or the incredible Creator?
If we choose to believe in the Creator,
Amazingly, He responds to our faith,
And our faith becomes a knowing.
Incredible, impossible—
But wonderfully true!

19. Beyond Measure

Beauty has no size—
A sky-full, a puddle-full of sunset,
Horizon curve, a bubble-bend of rainbow,
A symphony, a laugh of glad surprise—
Beauty has no size.

Happiness has no time—
The gentle rhythm of a life of love,
The overflow of moments into memories,
The sudden burst of joy that lights eternity—
Happiness has no time.

Faith has no definition—
It soars beyond reason,
Persists without proofs,
And blossoms into miracles—
Faith has no definition.

20. Coincidence

Two things never change:
Not the world or a star,
But two standards of measure
To show how great things are.

Predictable is the speed of light—
Distance is measured in light years,
Or the seconds to print a picture,
Or timed light to alleviate fears.

Almighty God, Who changes not,
Measures man by the light of His Word.
Clothed in glorious Light
He is hid from our sight,
But His standards of light we have heard.

His Word says, "God is Light,
And in Him is no darkness at all."
Yet the life He created depends
On His created Light to live at all.

Since God created Life and Light,
And Light sustains Life though the Son,
Could it be a coincidence
That these two changeless Powers are One?

21. God Beyond Measure

One man wrote wisely, "Your God is too small,"
But the God I worship is not small at all!
When He planned and created Time and Space,
He must have been working from some other place.
Though He created the universe, and is in it,
Surely what He created is not His limit.

He knows all my thoughts, and places some there,
(He knows all men's thoughts everywhere.)
He designed all our systems, keeps them working, too,
And that's probably simple for Him to do.

Overseeing our history and present is insufficient,
So He also knows and plans the future.
That's more than omniscient.

As scientists probe the edges
Of the universe God designed,
Measuring distances with the constant
Of the waves of light they find,
They determine ages of the past
With time of elements' decay,
Predict demise of the earth
A long time away,
But understanding of eternity
They don't attempt to convey.

I know God is awesome, powerful and wise,
He lives eternally in infinite skies,
And even His love of His creation,
Good or bad, I can see,
But though I accept, I don't understand
His intimate love and care for me.

Chapter VI

Why Do You So Long to Save the Lost?

1. A Way, Ways, and the Way

Why do people try so hard
To find another way to eternal life,
Ignoring or rejecting the Way
God has provided in His Son?

Meditation and Eastern religions
Promise an impersonal oneness,
Or nothingness.
What kind of eternal life is that?

Rules and self-discipline
May lead to perfection;
But what God promises
That goodness or self-perfection is enough?
And whose definition of perfection?

Is giving of one's time or money
To help those in need the way?
Who sets the guidelines and limits?
Who judges the motives of the heart?

Love, just love—Is that the way
To life eternal?
Is that the standard set?

Fame and money, service and courage,
Inventions, accomplishments, and wisdom
May win memorials or historic name,
But is that and eternal life the same?

In His love for His created man,
God made a Way, the only one,
For man to gain eternal life
In heaven with Him and His eternal Son.

It's simple, and easy enough to do
If you just can let go of you,
And in faith release control of self
Into the loving hand of our caring God.

The willful man won't give up control,
And at death must give up his very soul.
Why do people try so hard
To avoid God's Way to eternal life?

2. View from the Inside

On that fateful day when the sky turned black,
And God turned His face away,
Were your sins a part of that deadly load
Jesus bore, and washed away?

Was your sin-prone old man in Jesus Christ
As He bled on the cross and died,
Sin's penalty paying in full by death
Of God's Son, and all souls inside?

Had you made your choice to die with Him
As your Master and your Lord?
Has God in His timeless eternity
Placed you, saved, within Christ, His Son?

Were you in Christ Jesus that Easter morn
When God's power broke the bonds of hell,
And Christ Jesus rose, conquering death
For Himself, and all who in Him abide?

Are you seated in Christ in heavenly places,
Child of God, adopted forever?
Yet by His infinite power, Holy Spirit within,
Serving Him on earth for the while?

That's the mystery of God's eternal plan—
As we hear His Word and believe,
In love with grace, God places us in Christ
To die, be born again, and rise to live forever
In Christ

3. Long Before Time Began

In the beginningless eternity before time,
Imagine the flow of love from God Almighty
To His Word and back,
From Them to the Holy Spirit
Who responds with joy and overflowing Love
Until infinity is overwhelmed
With Love and Joy and Peace.
Where can it overflow?

Picture the sharing of ideas of beauty—
Light in all its variations
Of sunset sky, rainbows, sparkle and shadows,
Color, form and order, constellations of light,
Shapes in motion, growing, dividing
Into infinite repetitions of beauty,
And perhaps even life!
What if it were tangible?

If they wanted do it, how?
Brainstorming in the Trinity
Of planning, engineering, programming
Something in time and space—
Creating time and space inside eternity and infinity!

Then the desire for someone to enjoy,
Someone to share whatever they could create,
And even share that joy and love and peace
Reverberating around infinity.
What pleasure imagining
Someone to commune with Them!
Then came the considerations of "ifs"—
What if the created sharer had a will?
Would he want to commune with Them?
What would happen if he rejected his Creator?
If he just did not fit
Into the joy, beauty and peace of eternity?
Let's do it, decided the Creator,
And plan for any contingency.

Long before Time began,
Our Creator programmed in infinite detail
Progressions of forms and shapes,
Provisions for life and reproduction,
For responses to changes and attacks,

For room to grow and decide and err
And dream and seek and know their Creator—
And all Time was planned
Before one electron was set in motion.
And the end was planned,
Glorious, full of shared love, joy, and peace.

Infinite wisdom and knowledge
Foreknew each created being,
Planned beauty for his eyes,
Yearnings for his heart,
Challenges to help him grow.
Could not the Creator of the heavens
Create a red maple tree for me to see
Just when my spirit needed joy?
Or a rainbow in a dewdrop when I passed by?
Or a smile from a stranger? A call from a friend?
No detail is too trivial,
No problem is unsolvable
For our Almighty God, our Lord,
Our Creator, our Teacher and Comforter.
Nothing is impossible for Him;
And when I find the place of harmony
And unity within my Lord and Savior,
Nothing is impossible for Him in me.
I'm part of His plans,
Chosen before time began,
Provided for by infinite wisdom and love,
Recipient of joyous surprises
And surprising joys and strengths,
Destined to be with Him
In His infinity for all eternity,
Sharing His overflowing joy, love and peace.

4. Oh, That Man Would Listen!

Oh, Man, why do you think I pour out My love to you,
Even sending My Beloved Son
To suffer and die for you?
Why am I so long-suffering and full of mercy?
Why do I chastise you
And send My prophets to warn you?
Why have I given you My written Word to guide you?

Do you not realize that this life is but testing,
A screening time for each of you
To determine which will choose
To spend eternity with Me?

And have I not told you of the eternal hell,
The torment in the Lake of Fire
For those who reject My love and mercy?
Do you believe My happy Words
And doubt My judgments?
Will you remember too late
That you must be either for Me or against Me?
That you have been created free to choose,
But that there is a choice to be made?
That your soul will live forever
Either way?

My heart aches for the willful blind,
The worldly ones with their empty gods,
Those who settle for science and philosophy,
For prosperity, security, gaiety,
Who prostitute themselves for momentary pleasure,
For the ignorant and uninformed,
For those who call My Name, but do not know Me,
Do not even believe My Word,
Or seek My power of grace,

Those who disobey,
Those who profane My Name—
For I love them, too,
And sent My Son to die for them, too—
And I know their hearts,
And see their eternal writhing in regret.

Oh that Man would listen!
Oh that they would choose Life!

5. Priorities

Tenderly you watch over me, my love,
Providing for me gloriously,
Guarding against any lack or hurt,
As long as I may live.
Your love warms me and blesses me.

How concerned you are lest I not know
The records, laws, and traps,
Or set foolish priorities and lose
The security you've sought.
I would not violate your trust.

But, Love, how your priorities
Focus on the few short years!
What about Eternity? Please take the time
To plan for life beyond these earthly years.

Dear Love, I'd gladly give this earthly wealth,
And yes, my very life for you,
To know your soul will live
In Him Who died for you and me.
Eternal Life is my priority.

6. No Comfort

No comfort, no consolation, only pity
For him who rejects Jesus as Savior and Lord:
For hell is as certain for him as death.

Does the world call him "good"?
Is he smug in his righteousness?
In willful ignorance rejecting revealed Truth,
Does he satisfy his soul with logic?

None is without sin, no, not one.
And the wages of sin is death,
Spiritual death—in hell.

Does he claim no sin?
Has he never put any person or thing
Before the Lord God Almighty?
Or spoken the Lord's Name in vain?
Or, in pride, claimed prerogative
To be his own god, determining right and wrong?
Or hated, resented, refused forgiveness to any?
Or stolen, even an hour of time from his employer?
Or told a lie—white, pink, or black?
Or lusted, or envied? Coveted?
Let him consider carefully,
For one sin, one little sin, condemns eternally.

Unless, unless . . .

There is a Way provided at great cost,
In great love and mercy,
One Way,
Jesus.

It is not too late.
He loves that man, and died for him.
Let that man reach out and receive
The freely-given gift of eternal life.

Or else,
No comfort, no consolation, only pity.

7. Your Day in Court

You will have your day in court,
More sure than the rising sun,
When you'll stand before your awesome Judge
To account for the things you've done.

The books shall be opened, the Book of Life,
To see if your name is there,
And the record book of your thoughts and deeds;
You'll agree that the Judge is fair.

If your name is in the Book of Life,
Your deeds of straw shall be stripped away
With the fire of your Savior's eyes,
But the gold and silver shall stay.

A thousand years later—a terrified wait—
Come the rest to the Great White Throne.
Their names are not in the Book of Life:
The Judge knows they are not His own.

They'll know their sin in rejecting Him,
See their thoughts and deeds revealed,
No excuse or regret can avail then,
No rebellion or sin concealed.

The time for choices is over soon:
We have but one lifetime to choose,
And eternity in the Lake of Fire
Is the fate of those who lose.

You shall have your day in court
As sure as the sun shall rise,
And you'll know your place in eternity
By the fire in your Savior's eyes.

8. You Stubborn One

God knows you, you stubborn one.
He knows your heart:
You know that God exists,
That He created the world and man,
That He gave you your brain—
And expects you to take it from there.

Maybe you even know He loves you,
But would you read His Word
To find out why?
To know His will?
You haven't time.
Would you try to talk to Him—and listen?
That's foolish, you think.

God has a plan for you,
Even you, you stubborn one.
He has prepared a place for you
In heaven, in His Son Jesus Christ,
That in the ages to come
You might give pleasure and glory to Him
Who created you and made the Way
For you to be redeemed from sin,
And live eternally with Him.

But God also has a place for you
If you do not choose to serve Him,
A place where you will never see His face,
Where you will regret for all eternity
Your stubborn independence.

Yes, you are predestined for heaven or hell,
But the choice is yours.
God loves you, has even died for you,
Paying the inevitable penalty for sin
So that you won't have to.
He loves you, woos you, longs for you,
But He will not force you.
You are predestined for Heaven or Hell,
But the choice is yours.
You stubborn one,
Is independence from God
Really worth the price,
You stubborn one?

9. Guilty

Guilty.
Yes, I was guilty.
I had tried to be good,
But there was that touch of rebellion,
That curiosity to know what it would be like.
And I did it, and wasn't even sorry—
Until I met the Man who had never sinned.

Little sins—Is there a little sin?
A little lie, a little forbidden fruit,
A deliberate refusal, a hidden resentment—
Yes, I was guilty.

And then I learned the penalty:
"The wages of sin is death,"
No maybe, no conditions—death.
What would it be like to be dead—forever?

He knew.
And knowing, He offered to die for me.
He took my sins, every single one.
And He was condemned and put to death for me.
He suffered the agony of hell for me.
He gave up the presence of the Eternal God, for me,
So that I could live forever.

Hallelujah!
Hell could not hold Him;
Death could not overcome His righteousness,
And He arose, alive and perfect—
No sin, no illness, no death.

And now He invites us, from His exalted place,
To put our confessed sins upon Him,
To put our illness and weaknesses upon Him,
And die with Him,
So we can rise with Him in new life,
And live with Him and our Father.
Because we believe in Him,
In His life as God's only begotten Son,
That His death on the cross was for us,
That he arose and is seated at God's right hand,
We are forgiven, placed in Him, abiding with Him,
Reborn in God's image, with new hearts.
God loves us that much, to send His Son to die for us.
He protects us, forgives us, leads us;
He sent His Holy Spirit to live in us.

And Jesus is preparing a place for us
To live eternally with Him
In the glorious presence of our Father.
He's coming for us, perhaps soon.
For us, the redeemed, forever has already started,
And we are His forever.

10. Arms to Fill

Dear friends,
Hold out your arms;
I want to fill them full of wonderful things:

Fountains of Love,
Rainbows of promises,
Oceans of Peace,
Sun-sparkles of Joy,
The Roadmap of the Way,
And Faith to move mountains and climb to heaven.

I want you to know Jesus, alive and with you,
And you abiding in Him,
Believing He is God's Son
Who paid your debt of sin with His precious blood.
I long for you to obey Him as your Lord,
Rejoice in Him as your Savior, your Strength,
Your Wisdom, your Shepherd, and your Eternal God.

I long for you to know God
As your heavenly Father, your Daddy,
Knowing His Love is yours forever,
Filled with awe at His Power, His Righteousness,
His Holiness, His grace and mercy.
I long for you to be filled with His Holy Spirit,
Comforting, guiding, teaching you,
Leading you into all Truth.

I want you to know God's Living Word,
Full of Truth and mystery,
Commands and promises, Guidance and warnings,
And glimpses of future times and eternity.
I hope you will learn to use God's Word,
Powerful as a two-edged sword,
A seed that God promises will grow.

It's too much for arms to hold,
So I'll put my wishes into prayer,
And let God give these gifts to you,
For with Him, nothing is too difficult.
All of these things are yours—
They come with Jesus.
You must learn to receive them,
For every promise of God is "Yea and Amen."
Spend time with Him in praise, worship and prayer—
For, "In the Presence of the Lord is fullness of Joy."

11. Jesus Wept

When Jesus looked over the world
He had died to save,
He saw so many who did not know Him
And His mighty Word of love,
So many suffering pain and sorrow,
Trapped in sin and ignorance.
And He wept.

"Ye have not because ye ask not"—
"Oh that ye would ask and receive."
Pray, my brothers, that our Father
May do His mighty works in each of us in need
In all the world, and that His perfect will be done.
Ask, and receive. He waits—and weeps.

12. When Does New Life Begin?

When did my new life with Christ begin?
Was it when the Holy Spirit overflowed my heart
With Joy and Love, Peace and Power,
That moment when I knew that Christ Jesus
Died and lives for me,
That in Him I live and breathe and have my being?

Or was it when I asked Him
To be my Savior and my Lord
At 10 or 12, 22, or 44,
Not knowing it was done?

Or was it the seed planted long ago
In Calvary, Pentecost, and Christmas?

Or could it have been before Time began,
When God Almighty chose me and you and you
To be His children, and live eternally with Him
If they would choose to be His own
In faith and willing obedience?

What if, in independence and pride,
I had chosen my own way, not THE Way,
And discovered my eternal soul
In darkness, with unending remorse
For disdaining the Truth of Christ,
With eternal spiritual death,
And no new life at all?

13. Kaleidoscope (Tricks with the Light)

Longing for the Light,
We follow any glimmer, like fools.
Then, to augment our vision,
We grasp the offered tool.
Ready always with deceptive lure,
Satan offers his kaleidoscope,
Showing lovely patterns to our sight
Which we mistake for Light.

He does it all with mirrors
Reflecting the same old lies,
Worthless fragments of glass
Broken eons ago with the Truth.
"Ye shall be as gods," he said to Eve,
"Knowing good and evil." And she ate,
Trading the presence of the One True God
For Satan's kaleidoscope of artificial glory.
"Go on, taste it; enjoy yourself,
No harm in it." And there was death.
"God is everything, in all and all in Him,
All one essence, an impersonal power of force."
And the little broken pieces of glass
Distorted the image of the living God
Who loves and gives and forgives.

"God is within each soul, so meditate
And look within until you merge with
The universal all, the cosmic consciousness."
So we look within until we find
The awesome illusion that we are gods,
And worship self, and not the One True God
Who will allow no other god before Him.
It's another sliver of glass to color the illusion.

"Since God is good, and God made everything,
And is in everything, there is no evil,
Except that which man determines is evil."
And so we rationalize away the sin
That damns us to eternal separation from God.
Lies, lies, all lies straight from Hell!

"And there is no life after death.
This life is all there is, so enjoy."
Another glob of glass to camouflage.

"Jesus was a good man
Who had the Christ-Consciousness that recurs
Throughout all time in every great man of God,
And is available to everyone who meditates on Truth."
"There are many paths to Truth."
And another bright red lie
Replaces the precious blood of Jesus Christ
With worthless glass.

Turn the kaleidoscope to see the lovely patterns—
Hinduism, Islam, Yoga, TM or Est,
Jehovah's Witnesses, Armstrong's Church of God,
Unity, Spiritualism, Scientology, on and on,
All built on the same old lies,
The same shifting bits of broken glass,
Reflected into fascinating illusions of the Truth,
Ending with frustrations and death.

But the Light is real,
And still we long for Light.
"Ye shall know the Truth
And the Truth shall make you free."
"I am the Way, the Truth, and the Life;
No man cometh unto the Father but by me."

"He sent His Word and healed them."
"Faith cometh by hearing,
And hearing by the Word of God."
"Him who cometh to me, I will in no wise turn aside."
"Seek, and ye shall find."

God has placed the telescope of the Word in our hands
That we may see Him and His Messiah,
The Light of the World.
There is no other way than Jesus Christ,
And His blood shed for remission of our sin.
God has given us the microscope of His Holy Spirit
To reveal the subtle Truth of His Word,
To show us our need for forgiveness,
The answer to our every need:
He speaks of Jesus to our hearts.

We long for the Light, and Jesus is the Light.
The Word is a lamp unto our feet.
Let us never settle for the deceiver
With his kaleidoscope of shattered glass—
Disproven lies that snare the careless.

14. The Only Way

Almost two thousand year have passed
Since that awesome Revelation was written:
God's judgment on a wicked world.
Has God changed His mind about sin?
Has His love and mercy for His imperfect man
Lessened the penalty of death for lies,
For adultery and homosexuality unrepented?
In His Word, He said:
"I am the Lord; I change not."
And "No man is righteous, no not one."
And "The wages of sin is death."

But yet, He has also said that He
"So loved the world that He sent
His only begotten Son, that the world
Through Him might be saved."
And the Son told us in His Word,
"I am the Way, the Truth, and the Life:
No man cometh unto the Father but by Me."

Is there, after two thousand years, another way?
Was that horrible death on the cross
Unnecessary?
Has God decided that good men of any faith
Are worthy of His heaven, without Christ?
Has He changed His definition of sin?
Is repentance enough without accepting Christ?
Or is modern man simply trying to remake
God in a kinder image to allow for sin?

If God is indeed eternal and infinite,
Creator of time and space, and man,
His Word, too, is eternal and does not change.
Today, as always, Jesus is the Way,
The only Way to eternal life.

15. Oh, How We Need Easter!

Oh, how we need Easter!
As in Jerusalem nearly two thousand years ago,
The darkness threatens to engulf the light.
In our circles of light we pull family and friends
Tight around us,
Hoping to keep them safe from the dark.

Must we fear the dark?
Remember that Dark can never conquer Light:
Easter is the triumph of Light over Darkness.
And Jesus, the Light, is inside us.
Let's share the Light that conquers Darkness,
Joyfully, confidently, boldly.
The battle was won on Easter.
Oh, how we need Easter!

16. Your Easter

Whose death and resurrection
Do you celebrate this Easter?
A Jewish prophet?
Jesus of Nazareth?
Redeemer? Savior?
God's Son Who died for our sins
And rose again, and lives forever?
God's miracle plan of salvation?
Of course.

But is it yours?
Was your sin-debt paid in full
When Jesus died?
Did your old, sinful man die
And a new one be born again,
Resurrected in Christ Jesus?
Did Jesus die for you,
And rise for your eternal life?

In thanks and praise
That God loved you so much
That He sent His Son to die for you,
And offer you eternal life with Him,
Celebrate your very own Easter.

17. Jesus Is Coming Again

Expectancy is in the air;
Excitement mounting everywhere;
Jesus is coming again.

For our sins born to die
Then arise to the sky,
Jesus is coming again.

Are you in Christ by faith in the Word,
Knowing Jesus as your Savior and Lord?
Jesus is coming again.

Wear God's gift of His robe of righteousness white,
Get ready for your rapture flight.
Jesus is coming again.
Trim the wick, your lamp prepare;
Be sure your oil of the Spirit's there;
Jesus is coming again.

In His Word He foretold the signs of that day;
Each one is fulfilled; what more need we say?
Jesus is coming again.

Gather your loved ones into the ark
Lest they be in the world when tribulations start.
Jesus is coming again.

As Light of the World, bid the sinner repent
Before God's time of grace is spent.
Jesus is coming again.
As He promised, He's coming again.
He's alive, and He's coming again.

18. God Did It All

The Almighty God, two thousand years ago,
Launched His Communication Satellite
To broadcast His Good News
To a lost and beloved world.
He empowered it with His Son,
The Eternal Light of the World.
The message multiplied:
God has done it all.
It is finished.
Christ's blood has done it all.
Jesus Christ as Savior, as Lord,
As Son of Man and Son of God,
Has done it all—to forgive our sins,
To show us our loving God,
To offer us forgiveness and Life Eternal
With Him and our Father, the Eternal God.

The Good News goes out in hundreds of tongues,
Into every country, into every open heart,
Night and day, year after year,
The Word spreads and works His wonders.
Turn on your receivers and listen!
God did it all two thousand years ago.
It's yours! Just believe and receive
Forgiveness, salvation, life eternal!
Hallelujah!

Chapter VII

Why Do You Give Us a Choice?

1. One Question

One question, only one
You must answer; then it's done.
You're free to choose, win or lose.
How to answer? Yes or no.
When? Now or then. Where? Here or there.

You didn't know? It can't be so!
The heavens declare; it's everywhere.
You know it's true deep inside of you.

You have surely heard at least one word!
In all the world the fame of that precious name
Called for at least one look in that precious book.

Your life is for a choice to respond to His dear voice.
Believe, and rightly choose; only doubters will refuse.
Faith offers you new life—doubt assures eternal strife.

God has offered you a way—
Don't harden your proud heart today.
If you won't believe Him now,
In that day you will have to bow.
One master only can you serve:
Choose Him who can your life preserve.
There is one question, only one,
To answer before your life is done.
Do you in Jesus, your Savior believe?
As Lord of your life, His forgiveness receive?
To make that choice is why you're here:
So that your name in God's Book of Life will appear.

2. Gambling

How much would you bet that your soul will not die?
Would you bet your life? Not I.
How sure are you that there is no hell?
Are you sure there is no heaven as well?
Would you bet your eternity that God is a myth?
Or that any old god is enough to deal with?

What are the odds that sin is O.K.?
Or that doing your best is an acceptable way?
That God's Word doesn't mean what it seems,
And your own righteousness is all that redeems?
"It is given unto man once to die, and then,
The judgment," is God's decree for men.

Will you bet your life that Jesus lied
When He said that for your life He died?
When He claims to be the only Way,
Will you reject His Word and salvation today?
Will you bet your life that God's Word is a lie?
Choose eternity in hell the day that you die?

3. To a Young Man

No pride of ancestry be thine,
(And yet it is a noble line.)
Live for the day, no regret, no fear,
And rejoice in those who brought you here.
The first birth may make you wise or clever,
But you must be born again to live forever.

4. We are Old, My Love

We are old, my Love,
And Death is lurking in the shadows.
Stay in the Light, my Love.
We've been one, my Love,
For nearly fifty golden years,
May it be forever, too?

If Death can part us, Love,
Then let us never die.
Join me in Christ, and live forever.
Could my joy in heaven
Be full without you, Love?
How could I let you go?

How could you choose, my Love,
To spend eternity in darkness
Without God—or me?
I know in faith, My Love, you've chosen
Christ as Savior and your Lord,
And in Him we'll be together in Eternity.

5. Indivisible

Without my spirit, my body dies—
It may look the same; there it lies—
But without the spirit, an empty shell
With the life of it in heaven or hell.

Without our God, our nation dies—
It may look alive, deceptive lies—
Defenseless without His protective hand,
Indivisible, God and our glorious land.

6. Which Way Will You Go?

Which way will you go in the years ahead?
At 16 the choices begin.
Will you drift along without a choice?
That way you can never win.

Will you work toward wealth or wisdom?
Grab for power, or strife?
Or let fleshly pleasures rule you?
Which road is your choice for life?

The narrow way may be lonely,
But it leads into the Light,
And Jesus goes with you every day,
And His Holy Spirit guides you aright.

For the choice is really death or life—
God made the options clear,
And the reward is great—eternal life,
With His peace and joy right here.

7. Once We Were Free

Once we were free in America;
We knew the Truth, and it set us free.
We declared that Truth self-evident;
We, the people, died so that Truth could be.

On the Word of Truth we based our law
With no king other than Christ our Lord,
And became one nation under God,
Inspiring the oppressed all over the world.

What pride kidnapped freedom away from Truth,
Assuming men, not God, authored Liberty?
What greed lured our leaders to their own way,
Forsaking Truth for insanity?

Once we were free in America,
Prosperous and protected, under Christ our King.
Now fear, pride, greed and lust fight to rule
While the freedom we cherish has a hollow ring.

We can still be free in America;
One Way, one Truth can set us free.
In Christ each is free, one nation under God,
Indivisible, in liberty, we can choose to be

8. Master Control

The wonders of science
That delight the mind
Are God's pre-planned patterns
For patient thinkers to find.

The One Who designed systems
And empowered man
Also designed us as His sons
In His master plan.

But perfect love
Will not force our stand—
Each man's master control
Is in his own hand.

As a tool will do nothing
Without program and power,
So a wise man seeks God's Way;
Then his genius can flower.

9. Shining Path

Don't follow every shining path,
Oh searching little bug.
The glowing way may lead nowhere,
But be just the slime of a little lost bug.

The Shining Path in China and Peru
Entrapped the blinded soul
With broken promises, empty dreams,
In the hopeless darkness of the whole.

God's Light, provided for our path
Through His Word and Spirit within,
Is a lamp to guide our willing feet
To the Way from the dark world of sin.

10. Chosen

Not a respecter of persons, our God,
But a chooser, a setter of standards,
A regarder of ways, a searcher of the heart.

He received and honored Abel's sacrifice,
But rejected Cain's, because he did not "do right."
Ishmael He blessed, but Isaac He chose and blessed.
He passed over the first-born Esau
To honor Jacob, the "Grabber"
With the Messianic line.
Why?
Why David over Saul?
Solomon over Absolom?
Why you? Why me?

Chosen: We have been chosen by God
Before the foundation of the earth.
I chose to respond.
Am I chosen because I chose to respond?
Soul, study to show thyself approved.

11. Consider Jesus

Consider Jesus—Whom do you see?
Only a man in history?
Is the babe at Bethlehem He?
Is He the teacher of Galilee?
Or the healer that made the blind to see?
Is He the Messiah of prophecy?
The servant Who suffered those stripes for me?
Who gave His life for mine on Calvary?
Paid His life for my sins, to set me free?
Did His death conquer Death in victory?

Consider Jesus—
Was thirty-three years—or eternity—His life span?
Swaddling clothes in a manger, naked on a cross,
Seamless white robe for which soldiers tossed,
Or is radiant splendor of Light His array?

Consider Jesus—Who is He to you?
Is He the Way, the Truth, the Life?
Living water? Manna? The sword for our strife?
Your Rock, your Fortress,
Your strength when you're weak?
The Word you feed on, the wisdom you seek?
Your Savior, your Lord, your God and your King?
The joy of your heart, the song that you sing?

Consider Jesus, at God's right hand enthroned,
Ever making intercession for His own,
Who lived and died and lives evermore
So that you can have life eternal in store.
Only in Jesus, Savior and Lord,
Can life eternal be found—
Each man must choose: there's no middle ground.

Consider Jesus—always loving you so.
Longing to save even when you say no.
His love, my prayers—we'll not let you go.
What joy, peace and love in Jesus you'll know!
Ignoring the question is answering "no".
Consider Jesus.

12, What Is Freedom?

Freedom is a treasure above price,
Rare indeed, and transitory,
With many imitations
That glitter and entice,
But disintegrate with time.

Freedom is a choice:
At great price, with divine cost,
We have been set free
From every bondage of the world,
Free to choose our masters,
Or our Master.

Freedom is a gift
Purchased with a Life a Death,
And a Resurrection.
It is freely given to everyone who asks,
But is not for sale at any price.

Freedom is dangerous,
For if man calls himself his master,
His knowledge is too limited,
His wisdom is too foolish,
And his will too weak
To avoid the traps and snares
Of the world, the flesh, and the devil.

Freedom is an illusion,
For if a man does not master himself,
He will find himself in bondage
To passions, ambition, pride, lust,
Money, or lack of money.

Yes, freedom is a gift—
Gladly receive it from the nail-scared hands;
Joyfully offer it again to Him
Who is alive forevermore,
To yield in obedience to His loving will—
And then, yes, then in obedience,
In Him be secure forevermore.
There is freedom.

13. Election

Where would we be without Jesus?
Look around this world and see
The nations that close out Jesus
Are where people long to be free.

See in the godless corners,
Ghetto or mansion, the empty joy
Where men worship, instead of Jesus,
Money, drugs, violence, or grown-up toy.

This year we voted for Jesus,
Though the ballot didn't list His Name,
But the subconscious wisdom of millions
Knew the issue just the same.

For Jesus is the difference
Between failing nations and our USA.
By ignoring the Source of our freedom,
We almost gave it away.
We need Jesus every minute:
Without Him, man can't be free.
Lord, be the Lord of our nation;
Lord, be the Lord of me.

14. The Will

All our earthly goods we leave to those we love,
Blood of our blood, flesh of our flesh,
Into whom we have poured our time and care,
Our love and prayer.

We leave the values we have taught,
The lessons we have learned,
And, yes, the mistakes we've made,
Our virtues and our faults,
Our prejudices and our faiths.
"No thank you," they may say.

But the treasures of my life,
The one thing worth living for,
I cannot will to them.
It must be sought and found
By each one for himself.
It is joy unspeakable and full of glory,
Peace that passes understanding,
Love that conquers over all,
And everlasting life with Him
Who is all love, joy and peace,
All righteousness and wisdom,
All justice, power, and glory.
Worthless all the earthly goods,
Worthless the worldly wisdom
Without the Giver of all gifts,
The Lord of Life Eternal.

My will is that those I love
Will yield their will to Jesus
In Whom is hidden all they seek, and more,
In this world and the next,
Eternity in heaven with God.

But they must choose.
I cannot force them to receive
Eternal Life, so freely given to those who seek.
I cannot close the gates of hell
To those who choose the world.
Their will determines their inheritance:
But I can pray.

15. No Room

When Jesus came into the world,
The world offered Him no room.
If He comes today, would we do more?
The royal suite, we presume.

When Jesus taught the Pharisees,
They gave His Word no room;
With the Word now He warns the wise;
They receive it gladly, we presume.

When the Truth was too much in Nazareth,
With stones they gave Him no room.
But we'd welcome His Truth anywhere,
Home, newspaper, schools, we presume.

(When it was time, Jesus died for us—
On Calvary, men found Him room—
And for prophet, dead, not a threat,
They found a rich man's tomb.)

Today, Jesus knocks at the door of your hearts;
Do you open and offer Him room?
Along with football, newspapers, TV,
There's time for Jesus, we presume.

When He comes in the air to call us home,
All of us who are His—and it may be soon—
Will the trumpet voice sound our names?
Or we learn that for us there'll be no room?

16. A Chance to Choose

What's the big deal about Easter?
The spring break from school is great;
A new outfit each year is nice,
As are jellybeans and chocolate eggs.
But do we ever join the Easter Parade?
We know who the Easter bunny is.
If Easter Sunday had never been,
Would it make any difference to us?
Would we still be living in hopeless despair
With shallow loves and hollow joy.
Seeking fame, wealth, or selfish sins that cloy?.
Easter gives us a chance to choose
A new Way of life, a nobler goal:
Our home and companion in eternity—
Either a defiant, fallen angel
With all he deceived,
Or a glorious, victorious Christ
With all who in Him believe.
It's Easter that gives us a chance to choose.

17. Never Let Them Know

Never let our school children know!
Don't ever teach them the truth
That God created their universe, their world,
And made men in His own spiritual image
To give Him pleasure and glory.

Don't teach them that they are sinners,
And that the wages of sin is death,
With eternal separation from God in hell.
We must be politically correct.
Never let them know!
It might make them afraid to sin.
Don't limit their freedom to think and act
By teaching them eternal truths beyond facts—
They must be free to choose in ignorance.

Don't tell them there are laws
Beyond math and science and government,
And that moral and spiritual laws
Are violated at their peril.
Don't let them discover that God, Who created them
Is a righteous God, their Judge and Jury,
Who requires faith and obedience,
And is worthy of praise.

Never let them know that God loves them
Enough to send His only begotten Son
To pay their penalty for their sins,
To die in their place,
And that He is eager to forgive with more than mercy—
But that even He cannot forgive
The sin of unbelief that rejects His forgiveness.
Don't tell them He gives His gifts of grace
To all who will receive, and more, much more,
According to His riches in glory.

Don't teach them that Jesus is the Way;
They need to learn that on their own,
And it might offend those who choose damnation.
Let them be free to decide
Which god to serve, which way is right,
And find themselves in hell for all eternity.

Don't ever let them know
That God's Word is the Truth
And has the answer to every problem.
Don't let the children know.
Never teach them the Truth,
It might confuse them.
They might reject the systems of the world,
And find Life Eternal.

18. A Living Soul

(Genesis 7:7: God created man
out of the dust of the earth,
breathed in him the breath of life,
and man became a living soul.)

"A living soul!"
God breathed into His created man
The breath of life,
And man became a living soul.

Into no other created being
Did God say He had breathed
His breath of life,
And yet they were all alive,
Even though all, too, were born to die.

Was it God's own eternal Life
He breathed into His man,
Created in His own image,
So that man's soul, like God's,
Would live forever?

Man, if your soul will live forever,
Should you not be concerned
About where that eternal life will be?
God gives us a choice,
And as for me, the choice will be
To live with God eternally in heaven.

19. One Unexpected Moment

In one unexpected moment,
Evil crashes planes of innocent people
Into tall buildings,
Full of unsuspecting businessmen.
The buildings shudder,
And burst into flames.
After a few moments of panic,
For the calling of loved ones,
And for some few to escape,
The stories collapse,
Top into next, one by one,
Into piles of rubble
Burying thousands of people.

So many lives snuffed out
In one unexpected moment!
So many lives disrupted,
A whole nation changed!
Unfinished dreams are gone.
Lives too short, too much to do—
Life doesn't end this soon!

Life doesn't end this soon—
Does it? Does the soul die with the body?
Or is death just a door into eternal life?
You knew, didn't you, that God gave you life
Here on this earth as a time to make a choice?

There are two doors that open at death,
One into the bright light and joy
Of eternal life with God in heaven,
And one into the darkness of hell,
With no more choice, ever.
In that unexpected moment,
Do you know which door will open for you?
Before that unexpected moment comes,
Make certain that you choose the Light.

Chapter VIII

Are You and Your Word Really One?

1. Proclaim the Word

Proclaim the Word!
God's Word has power—
    To create a world,
    To call out a people,
    To establish His law,
    To be born a Savior,
    To give man a new spirit,
    To establish a church,
    To prevail against the gates of hell.

We are set free from sin and death
To proclaim God's Word
So that others, too, may live.
Proclaim the Word!

2. Spaceship

Created out of God's faith by His awesome Word,
Our spaceship universe floats in infinity,
For a time borrowed from eternity,
Upheld by the Word of His faith.

Through the valve of the Word
Faith enters to create, planting seeds of the Word.
The Word became flesh and dwelt among us.
Only through Jesus, the living Word,
Is the Way for God's chosen who have chosen Him
To leave the confines of this universe,
Limited by time and space,
And enter the timeless, limitless ecstasy
Of their Father's eternity,
With, and in, their Savior, the Word.

3. Like the Word

Like the Word, this curved lens reaches outward
Enlarging our view in every way.
Like the Word, this lens reaches inward,
Sprinkling rainbows each sunny day.

Like the Word, this lens is a doorway
Linking worlds, without and within;
Like the Word, this is a sharing of God's love,
An instrument to view the world and show His glory.

4. Brushed and Braided

In the morning my mind,
Disheveled like sleep-tossed hair,
Needs to be brushed and braided.
With strokes of prayer and praise,
The brush of God's Word
Brings order to random thoughts.
Living water washes away the worries of the World,
And the oil of the Holy Spirit enlivens and grooms.
The Word organizes and directs.

And as I meditate on my Lord, the Living Word,
Filled with the Spirit of the Living God,
As I lift my heart in joy to God my Father,
The weak strands of ordered thoughts
Are braided together with the Spirit and the Word
Into the triple-strength of blessed order and unity.
Ready to be a crown of glory in His service.

5. God's Promises

God's promises are forever—
He's never broken one:
As our Way to receive these promises,
He gave us His promised Son.

In the Garden of Eden God promised
Redeemer and Conqueror, too,
To overcome Adam's trespass,
Make His plan of a kingdom come through.

To Noah he set His bow in the sky
As a sign as the waters recede;
To Abraham God promised to bless
The whole world through his seed.

Moses, David, Isaiah—all of God's prophets—
Planted His Word,
Picturing completely our Messiah
Before news of Christ's birth was heard.

And Jesus fulfills every promise
God has given of His Son,
Sinless and faithful until death,
Alive, Savior for everyone.

Jesus' promises are forever—
He's never broken one;
With God He sent the Holy Spirit
To assure each promise be done.

And lo, He is with us always
To strengthen, teach, and love
Until He calls His own to come
To spend eternity with Him above.

For God's promises are forever.
There's no failure in His plan
To fellowship in heaven forever
With His children—redeemed, born-again man.

6. The Pleasant Land of Thy Word

Oh Lord, I love to linger
In the pleasant land of Thy Word.

I visit the Patriarchs and prophets
Living on faith in a barren land,
Receiving Thy spoken Word, Oh Jehovah,
Discovering in their need
Thy vast variety and changeless strengths,
Finding firm the steadfast ground of Thy promises,
The harsh realities of straying sinners,
Thy mercy that endures forever.

In the telescope of prophecy I see—
A hint here, a picture there, a type—
My Lord the Christ planted in the Word
By Eve and Abraham, David and Solomon,
Isaiah, Daniel, Amos, Joel, and all to John.
Then they add to history their visions
Of Jesus, our Savior, our soon-returning King.

I sing the Psalms with David
As he rests secure with Thee among angry enemies;
I dance with him as he brings the Ark
Into God's chosen resting place,
And with David confess my bitter sins,
Unwilling to live without Thy Spirit,
And lay my soul bare, asking forgiveness,
So glad I know the Author and Finisher of my faith,
And the greatness of Thy love, Thy grace.

I love to sit with Mary at the feet of Jesus,
Listening to His wisdom, warmed by His love.
In awe and utter humility
I stand with His mother and John,
And watch His precious blood pour out for me,
And, both sad and glad, feel my sins washed away.
I'm among the 120 at Pentecost
Praising, worshipping, rejoicing with one accord;
I see the tongues of fire, and feel one warm my spirit,
And so overflow with love and praise
That torrents of living water pour out in unknown tongues.
With Paul I trace the task our Lord blessed,
Learning the challenge, the joys and heartaches
Of Thy great commission,
The Source of strength, the nature of the struggle,
The bogs and pitfalls and tempters,
The greater reality of faith
Over so-called realities of the world.

I gather a bouquet of Thy promises,
Putting them in the vase of faith,
Filled with living water.
There's always room for one more.

Then with the wonder of Thy Living Word,
I step into my place prepared in Christ
And speak Thy promises into reality,
And live within the pleasant land of Thy Word.

7. Perfect Parts of a Perfect Whole

Oh Lord, my God, Lord God Almighty,
Your Word is a perfect whole,
Altogether lovely:
Wide, wide beyond horizons to infinity,
Deep, deep, layer upon layer,
Rich, with infinite varieties of treasures,
Wise, baffling geniuses, delighting the faithful,
Holy, awesome, fearful in holiness,
True, eternally true with no compromise,
Powerful, with unassailable power,
Loving, self-giving, unending love—
All in one indivisible harmony,
Altogether lovely,
And His Name is Jesus.

And yet, within the perfect whole of Your Word
Are exquisitely patterned, perfect parts
Like CAT-scan art panels in every direction.
Picture the fruit of the Spirit
From Genesis to Revelation,
Or covenants old and new,
Or the dark, strong tones of judgment,
Side by side
With the sunshine colors of forgiveness.

Follow the scarlet thread of Jesus' blood,
Or the powerful Sword of the Spirit,
The Living Water, manna, or the Rock
Eternity will not yield time enough
To explore the infinite number
Of precious patterns and panels in the Word,
Or grasp the loveliness of the perfect whole.
Still, thank You, Father,
For giving us eternity to try.

8. Of Books and the Book

Books open doors to great new lands,
Or windows into great old minds,
Paint pictures, real or fantasies,
Or charicatures, portraits, subconscious finds,
Teach how to make or do or live,
To understand the world, or man,
The why's and how's and who's and when's,
Matters' beginning and its end—
If I could read sunset to sunrise,
Year in, year out, till life is done,
Each kind of book, would I be as wise
As if I'd studied God's special One?

We can learn from Thucidides
The history of Greece,
From Caesar the conquest of Gaul,
From Gibbon, of Rome and its fall,
From Sandburg of our Civil War,
From Churchill, of our world-wide fight—
But the Bible tells of the battle supreme
Between forces of evil and good,
And not only that, from beginning to end,
Not myth, but fact,
Not science fiction, but truth.

Biography? How many great men have been studied,
Word-pictured for us to know in and out?
Cleopatra, Socrates, Napoleon,
King Arthur, Elizabeth the Great,
Washington, Lincoln, Martin Luther King,
Madam Curie—the list's without end.
But without Moses and Joshua. David and Job,
Elijah, Esther and Ruth,
Without Abraham and Solomon, Jezebel—
Without Jesus, no list is complete.

Shakespeare and Chaucer, Dante, Racine,
Aristotle, Shaw—great worlds complete,
Depth, breadth, wisdom, and life.
But the Bible is more, for beside its pictures
Is the eternal reality, Life itself.
It contains truth, oh yes, but more—
It is Truth.
Within its pages, is all we need to know
Of life, history, philosophy, beauty,
Right and wrong, time and eternity.
For in it is the record of God's love affair with man.

Who has studied the Book is wise and learned;
Who has not read and studied it is ignorant.

9. Open Doors

Jesus says, ". . . Behold, I stand at the door and knock."
He does not enter uninvited,
But when we open the door of our hearts
And ask Him to come in,
We recognize Him and know that He is God
Who really did die for our sins.
In turn, He invites us to become part of Him,
His very body here on earth, to be redeemed.

Cleansed and renewed by His shed blood.
He asks us to share in all He has and all He is,
To serve Him and shout His Truth from our housetops.
Christ Jesus, the Word, the Way to eternal Life abundant,
Is the open Door to all we have ever yearned for.
What wondrous gifts He brings, gifts that keep on giving.
Rich beyond our dreams, sparkling our lives,
Enriching our souls and giving us new spirits
That opens doors into the very heart and mind of God,
Into His eternity and infinity.

And with our new spirits comes the Holy Spirit,
Gift of God to live within us.
As we become ready and willing, He shows us the keys
To open the secrets of life abundant and full of glory;
To discover the mysteries
In the depths and riches of God's Word;
To find treasures of Truth, Joy, Wisdom, and Love;
To experience the Power of His Word
That upholds the world, and lifts and keeps our souls.
Let us be bold to step through every door He opens,
To take time to meditate, and let the Truth soak in.
And then let us take up His Word, the Sword of the Spirit,
And step into new realms
In the infinite, eternal wealth of His magnificence.

Equipped with the powerful gifts of the Spirit,
And led by the Spirit into understanding and wisdom,
We are ready to go through the doors God opens
To share the gifts of salvation with others,
Showing them the wonders of opening doors,
Confident that we are in Jesus, and He in us,
That He has shared His very nature with us,
And asks us to share these open doors with everyone
Who needs an open door to life and our Eternal God.

10. Oh, the Starving People, Lord

Oh, the starving people, Lord,
How can we feed them all?
How can we focus into reality
All Your love and caring for each one?

Oh, the starving bodies, Lord,
Swollen, whimpering, hopeless—
And for fifty cents a day
We can channel Your love and life into one.

Oh, the starving minds, Lord,
Fooled with an empty education,
Clutching papers, despairing hollow minds,
How can we teach them wisdom, Lord?

Oh, the starving spirits, Lord,
Weak and ignorant of Your grace and love,
Or new-born and helpless in a wicked world
Without the might of Your Word!

Oh Lord, Who sent His Son to die for us,
Who planted His written Word for us,
Who sends His Spirit to live in us,
Forgive us for half-hearted service.

And help us, forgiven, as we offer ourselves
As channels for life-giving food
For starving bodies, starving minds,
And starving spirits, feeding all for You.
For You have provided food enough
For all Your creation,
Food for bodies, food for minds,
And Your glorious Word for spirits.

We, Your stewards, are culprits:
In pride, greed, laziness, or ignorance,
Depriving fair share to each,
Limiting growth of Christ's Body.

Come, Body of Christ, let us rally in Him.
With the sword of the Spirit,
The shield of faith, the joy of the Lord,
Let's feed the world: body, mind, and spirit.

11. God's Glad, Glorious Good News

Shout it from the housetops,
The glad, glorious Good News
That a Savior has been born!
Spread the Word. Find no excuse!

Tell a friend! Preach to crowds!
Write letters; send out scrolls.
Form a church, print pictures, sing,
Until the whole known world knows.

Persecution couldn't stop it.
God bypassed planned ignorance
Inspiring Gutenberg to print the Word
So that common men could understand.

In centuries the glad Good News
Spread world-wide to every nation,
But to speed it up, God inspired men
To telegraph, telephone His information.
Then radio, records, movies, TV,
Cable, satellite, and now Internet
Carry God's glad, glorious Good News,
Available for all the world to get.

Glorious Word! Innovative God!
Of course you've heard
God's glad, glorious Word.

12. The Wonder of the Word

Oh the wonder of the Word, the Living Word,
The Spoken Word, the printed Word, our Jesus.
He is the Word, a Lamp unto our feet,
The Light of the World, and the Way.

God's Word is a laser, a sharp two-edged sword,
He is a surgeon's scalpel, purifying, healing,
Cutting away sins and error, doubt and disobedience.
The Word is a fire, a laser beam, a weapon
In the battle against Satan and his servants.
He is a coiled wire, wound by God's power
Ready to spring into action
Whenever faith releases that power.
The Word is a battery of stored power
An eternal generator of electricity
Whenever the Believer makes the connection
And with prayer turns on the switch of faith.

The Word is a Rock, a never-failing foundation,
And building blocks, fitted without fault
Into an impregnable fortress.
It is the unchanging standard of measures
Used to test all other measures.

God's Word is Living Water patiently wearing away
Any boulder or belief challenging its power,
Seeping through walls, moving mountains,
Washing away dirt and stubborn pebbles.

Jesus, the Word, is Life, renewing the mind,
Quickening the flesh, preparing hearts to be born again,
Sustaining and feeding the new spirit
Until it matures into the likeness of God Himself.
He is manna, spiritual food, both milk and meat,
Perfectly balanced, nourishing and delicious.

The Word is a container of God's history,
His commands and promises, prophecies,
Proscriptions and prescriptions, warnings, examples,
Teachings, Truths, and mysteries.
Within the Word we can find success, avoid failure,
Praise and worship, glory and gore,
Philosophy, psychology, science.
There are pictures of all kinds of people,
Of the world, and heaven and hell.

All of these, and every Word is alive, full of power,
Ready to be released in faith
To accomplish that which God intended,
And return to Him fulfilled.
Jesus, You are the Word, the Living Word,
Spoken, written, eternal, and You are our Lord.

13. The Word

"In the beginning was the word,
and the word was with God
and the word was God." (John 1:1)
"And God said, 'Let there be light,
and there was light. (Gen.1:1)
"Meditate on the word day and night."

In the wireless Word,
The power of God creates a world;
He takes concept into concrete existence
Within His created time and space.

Through His Word, God planted His presence
In hearts of chosen people.
Through His Word, He nurtured it,
Adding illustration, guidance
In nature, in history, in philosophy.
In His written Word He stored it,
Tangible record of His ways and will,
Guidebook for His creation,
Storehouse of His Power on earth.

Although man has not quite understood how,
"The Word became flesh and dwelt among us,"
To show us the Way
From our dimensions of time and space
Into infinity and eternity.

Written or Living, the Word is God
Come into time and space,
A gate through which pass the thoughts of God
Into time and space,
Becoming tangible, finite,
Existent in time and space—
The Creator coming into His creation.

Even more, the ultimate more,
Absorbed in us, made central in our lives,
The Living, Spoken, Written Word
Can bring us out of time and space
Into infinity and eternity—with Him.

14. My Search for the Word

When I was a child all I knew of the Word
Were the thrilling stories I had heard.
I loved my Lord Jesus, all love and delight;
I'd be His sunbeam, reflecting His light.

Blood poisoning at twelve threatened amputation,
But the year disabled gave time for meditation.
I read the Word through, Elsie Dinsmore books—thirty,
Accepted the truth, unaware of all obscurity.

As a questioning teen, I wrote my own creed:
God was a name for unknowable, and answers we need.
While in college, all sure I was wise,
I scanned the good Book looking for lies.

I accepted the ethics, philosophy, too,
But Jesus, was He just an illegitimate Jew?
And yet, that man of Galilee,
Did He really die for me?
He changed the cross from shame to glory,
And for 2000 years, men have treasured His story.

At a Methodist youth camp, I made the decision—
I went to the altar, braving derision,
Invited Christ into my heart at twenty-one,
But in hours praying with me, no one said "It is done."

In tears and prayer, I awaited a sensation,
Getting none, God-rejected, thought the Word man's creation.
Never sure, yes or no, never wanting to doubt,
I put on a mask, afraid to find out.
I went to church, taught the youth,
Sang in choirs, prattled Truth.
Jesus? I knew much about Him
But never having met Him, I'd doubt Him.

Then, determined to find fraud or treasure,
I searched the Book with science as a measure;
Passing over the gold, I mined inconsistencies;
Missing pearl of great price, I chose ambiguities.

Three sons—baptized, Why not? Would it hurt?
Then with the eldest, I joined the church.
I was counted a Christian, with acceptable motions,
And overflowing with love, but hypocrite in devotions.

Once I met Jesus, after days of hyper mental activity,
But being on medication, I questioned the validity.
Yet my subconscious knew, and the search had begun—
I'd glimpsed joy in the presence of God's only Son.

With atheist Ayn Rand I viewed Objectivism,
But balked at her devastation of "Altruism."
For two years I pondered. Was it divine revelation
That finally showed me her faulty definition?
Kafka, Thomas Mann, Teilhard and de Nouy—
I sifted and searched, affirmed and denied.

Four years of teaching in a Christian college
Let me meet some of His, and crave their inside knowledge.
Hungry for the Word, I enrolled in Sunday school,
And we searched for Truth together, Bible as a tool.

Yearning, reaching for the illusive "Something More"
I read about the Holy Spirit, scoured library and store.
My learned friend received Him, Holy Spirit and the tongue,
And still was sane and reasoned, happier, inside young.

In a threesome prayer group, asking God to conquer fat,
We learned to yield, obey Him, repent of sins like that.
Cleansed of sin by His blood shed for us on the cross,
Forgiven, ready to count the world as loss,
We prayed in faith, believing in His perfect Word,
And with new tongues receiving, we knew that we were heard.

And now the Word is different—rich and full and strong—
And happiness is to study it all day, all my life long,
To walk with Jesus, the Living Word, to seek His perfect will,
To know the peace, the love and joy, His wishes to fulfill.

How sweet to know His presence in prayer and daily task,
How blessed to know He answers every prayer we ask.
How satisfying to serve Him, praise Him with a friend,
How wonderful to worship Him in life without an end!

I know He cares enough for me, despite rebellious mood,
To search for one lost sheep like me, give my spirit food
To keep me living, longing for the Lord I didn't know
Until my soul was ready to seek Him, begin to grow,
To realize He loves each one, will never let us go—
Lord Jesus, teach me to feed Your sheep and love them even so.

15. The Word of Power in Motion

With His glorious Word of power,
God set the world in motion.
He said, "Light, be!" and that brief Word
Established all sources of Light,
And sent its waving rays to conquer darkness
With the most distant star,
Or with the lighted match in your hand,
Light flowing at its constant speed,
Measuring distance with time.

With His Word of Power, God created
From things invisible all things seen,
Setting in motion electrons and protons
In carefully numbered patterns,
Combining them in pre-planned elements,
Holding them in circling tension with His Word.

With His Word of Power,
Working in wonderful wisdom,
God gathered together elements
In long, long lasting, self-feeding
Balls of fire, seething and sending,
In all directions, waves of light, heat, sound.
With ultra and infra waving rays,
Each wave with identifying, consistent patterns.
And with His Word of Power
He sent these balls in motion
With just the speed to keep the spacing
Constant, predictable,
To keep majestic galaxies swirling,
Expanding, sending out their light-waves,
All set in motion, held in order
By the Word of Power of Almighty God.

Swirling within our galaxy
Our solar system moves in its concentric circles
And oval comet paths around our sun,
With spin and orbit established
By God's creative Word of Power
Measuring the movement of time.

While the giant plates move the continents,
Pushing them up, shaking, breaking,
While sediment and molten rock shape,
And the weather cycles and rain erode,
Slowly moving and changing,
Scientists discover they are systems
Set in motion by the plan and Word of God.

And life itself is motion,
Seed growing in pre-planned patterns,
Like producing like in multiplying life.
There are systems within—reproductive,
Digestive, skeletal, circulatory, sensory, mental—
And systems without—social, family, business,
Government, civilizations—
And all are planned to work according to design
By laws proclaimed by God in His Word.
Beyond our sight, but not beyond our knowing,
God has set His kingdom in motion,
Planting the seed of His Word in the world,
Sending His Son to establish that Kingdom,
And gathering His body together
Through the Power of His Word.
He places new spirits in His own
And upholds His promises with His powerful Word.
His Word is growing within us and spreading,
Fighting and conquering,
Preparing us for eternity with Him,
All being accomplished by His glorious Word.

All glory and honor and power
To the Engineer-God Who designed,
Created, and set in motion
All things seen and unseen
With His glorious Word of Power.

16. John 14

Lord, I am what I am, and that's all I can be
Until You come and abide in me.
When You are in me, and I abide in You,
Then every Word of Yours can even in me be true.

Chapter IX

You're Serious about Commitment, Aren't You?

1. In Oneness of Desire

In Oneness of Desire
Like the puppy waiting at the door,
All tail-wagging joy,
To greet his beloved master;
With singleness of seeking as the hurt child
Runs to His mother to be comforted
By the tight security of her loving arms;
With the persistence of longing of the young wife
For her soldier husband away at war,
To melt into his returning heart in oneness;
I long for the joy of Your presence, Lord.
I rush to our special meeting
In the depth of my spirit,
The secret place of the heart created by Your love,
Opened by my repentance,
Cleansed by Your forgiveness,
Kept open and sacred in anticipation.
Come, Lord. I wait in longing and love.

Hallelujah!
You are already here!

2. Your Voice

Teach me to hear and know Your voice, Oh Lord,
  In my prayer,
  In my thoughts,
  In Your Word,
  In Your world.
For You have promised
That Your sheep know Your voice.
I am one of Your sheep—so happy to be one—
I hear Your voice.

3. Right with God

Oh, Lord, I want to be right with You.
Forgive me for neglecting Your Word,
Time with You in prayer and praise,
Procrastinating in visiting
And showing Your love to others—
Forgive me for everything.
Help me this new year
To put You first, always,
To be obedient and humble,
To serve where I am planted, with joy.
Help me to reach out to others
And show them You and Your Son.

4. Fountain of Living Water

Dear Lord, You give of Yours,
And give and give of Yourself.
And are not diminished.
Because You live in me,
Replenishing my spirit with Living Water,
I give and give of the bounty
With which You have blessed me,

And give and give of myself,
And I am not diminished.
You are within me a fountain of Living Water
That flows from my spirit in an endless river
Blessing and nourishing all who drink from it.

Because You are my Shepherd,
I shall not want.
I shall not and do not want
For time to meditate on Your Word,
For time to praise and worship You,
For time to fellowship with You,
For time to hear Your voice,
For time and will and strength
To obey Your every direction,
For wisdom to discover Your Way
Among the many ways,
For power over any enemy
That seeks to deter or undermine
Your will in my life and in Your Body.

5. Love

Love!
For God is Love; it's true.
When He is first within your heart,
His love is manifest through you.

6. Awakening

How patiently, how lovingly You wait, Oh Lord,
For us to awaken to Your Word.
You have poured out the eternal flow
Of Your blood for our salvation,
And we eagerly enter into the cleansing flow,
But selfishly fail to let the whole world know.

You have placed the precious promises
In Your Word,
And we peek into cracks and pick a few
Almost as if they were forbidden fruit.

You have poured out Your Spirit on the earth,
And Your own children, born again,
Hold out their thimbles or their cups.

Oh, Lord, let me not hold out a bucket,
Or a bushel or a barrel,
Or even a cistern
To hold the never-failing river of Your Spirit,
But let me—washed clean,
    Reborn,
    Yielded,
    In Christ,
    Abiding in the Word,
    Promise-packed,
    Spirit-filled—
Become a channel
For Your never-ending stream of Living Water,
To let the whole world know the wonders
Of Your Way, Your Word, Your will.

7. Because We Are His

Because we are His
Newborn in the Spirit,
And we want all to share,
We choose His symbol and wear it.

Because we are His,
We will walk in the Way;
However He asks us,
We will serve Him each day.

Because We are His,
One day at a time,
We release to His will.
Lord, may this servant be Thine.

8. Still Water Running Deep

Like still water, I must be quiet
To reflect the glories of my Lord:
The golden branches of love,
The peaceful green of eternal life,
The heavenly blue of His presence in my heart,
And always, the brilliant sparkle of His joy.
Be still, heart, and know that He is God.
Be still, mind, and listen to His voice.

But living water must flow,
Lest it collect the scum of complacency,
Lest it become brackish, self-centered.
Let my still surface reflect,
But let the current of Living Water flow
Constantly under those reflections
To carry the Living Water to others,
To offer itself up for others to drink,
And spread the Truth, the Life, and the Light
Throughout my little world.

And living water must receive,
Or drain away or evaporate.
Let there be rivers of Living Water
Constantly flowing into me,
Through the Living Water of the Living Word,

Through the Living Water of the Holy Spirit within
Bubbling up rivers of Living Water as I pray.
Let me be a channel of Living Water,
Still enough to reflect Your glory,
Ever flowing in Your chosen direction,
Always giving, never withholding,
But always being replenished,
Filled to overflowing.

9. It's Time to Simplify

It's time to simplify, to sort and choose
Which treasures of ours to hold, which to loose.
So many lovely baubles to move and dust around,
Extra shoes and dresses, lost for years, then found,
Books and tapes, each full of truth and beauty,
And piles of files and records, saved for wisdom,
    fun, or duty.
Now my hours slip through my fingers;
My body demands more rest,
And it's time to let go the lesser
To focus on the best.
There are still dreams to capture,
Eternal truths to share,
Friends and family to cherish,
Strangers who need my care.
Things become a burden, monopolizing time.
It's time to simplify my life,
To finish work God has assigned.
He's coming soon to call His own;
It's time now to prepare,
To be holy and robed in His righteousness.
Prepared for His presence there.

10. On Fire

Long years ago I saw my Lord,
And heard His loving voice;
His Word revealed a Father's dream
—For His Way I made my choice.
With heart on fire with love and joy,
I tried to share the flame;
Some friends were cool and comfortable,
Preferring to stay the same.

I could have sought another place
Where souls were hungry for the Word,
Where hearts could come alive with joy
In revelations of Truth they heard.

I've planted countless seeds of faith,
And seen good fruit from those that grow.
I've delighted in dear souls on fire—
Hungry to share in the Truth they know.

Dear Father, with such wondrous dreams
Of contagious faith with joy and power,
Of warriors skilled in the sword of Your Word,
Why are some of Your children so weak at this hour?

Why doesn't the Word make their hearts burst with joy?
Why don't they know that the victory's won
As soon as they rely on Your Word in faith?
In Christ all the conquest is done.

Some don't even know there's a war,
And that they are the army of God.
They are unaware of the hell that awaits
All not redeemed by His blood.

Did I miss Your war plan in where I fought?
Did I fail to listen to Your voice?
Or was I here in this luke-warm place
To plant seeds as the job of Your choice?

Your Word still sets my heart on fire,
And it wills obedience to Your call.
My desire, to serve as You command,
With my spirit, soul and body—my all.

11. Your Father's Love

Before you were born, even eons ago,
God chose you to be His very own,
Patterned your genes so you would grow
To do what He wanted done.

He has already planned what He will ask,
And is equipping you in talents required,
In wisdom and skills needed for each task,
And a heart to desire what He has desired.

His eternal rewards He has set aside
And inexpressible joys for you day by day
As you learn to listen, in His Word abide,
And let His Spirit guide you all the way.

As He lovingly watches your talents grow,
Finds your heart in tune with His Will and Word,
He'll touch you with His love, and you'll know
That it is really His voice you have heard.

He's proud of you, His child, as you meet each goal
With a heart and mind that are pure,
As you let the trials mold your very soul
With humble heart, and a faith that's sure.

12. Crew

As a member of the crew,
Selected one from many,
Strong in shoulders, arms and legs,
Each is perfectly committed
To a mind of strength,
Self under control,
Joyfully yielding to purpose,
One in unity.

One of many,
Chosen and tested,
Each is committing strengths
While freely melding into one,
Yielding to coordinating control,
Joyfully dedicating to one purpose,
One in unity.

Many in one Body, chosen before time began,
Developing strengths from weaknesses,
Learning self-control
By yielding to the Infinite One,
Each of us committing in His love,
Dedicating to His purpose,
Joyfully resting in His strength,
Invincible in His will,
One in Unity.

13. Living Trust

I'm setting up a living trust,
Investing for eternity,
Tax exempt, inflation-proof,
With God as its security.

A tenth of income I should include,
And add a tithe of time,
Plus sharing of the eternal Truth
In teaching and in rhyme.

Ready prayers for hurting souls,
With love and a listening ear,
And sharing goods with hungry men
Whose needs are now and here.

I'll add total commitment to my Lord,
Obedience to His will,
Faith in His Word, incessant prayer—
The investment is paltry, still.

I'll choose my Savior as Trustee,
And put all in His loving hand,
Confident of heavenly return
When in His presence I stand.

14. America, It's Time to Pray (National Day of Prayer)

America, return to God!
Lost in the glare of headlines
Shouting adultery and lies,
Corruption and greed,
Violence and selfishness,
Ethnic cleansing and grabs for power,
How can we focus on prayer?
How can we seek God for help
In reestablishing His values
In people who think He is dead?

Yet God always has His remnants,
Even in Sodom and Gomorah
God did not have even ten righteous men,
But did spare righteous Lot—
And his family, who were not.
When Moses returned from Mt. Sinai
To find the Israelites worshipping the golden calf,
The Levis were faithful.
Elijah, thinking he was the only one true to God,
In the wicked reign of Ahab and Jezebel,
Learned from God of 7,000 true to God.
Daniel and his three friends were true;
Isaiah and Jeremiah, Ezekiel and Joel,
And many, many more: God's men.

Overwhelming disasters swirl through our land,
Fires and floods, mud-slides and droughts,
Hurricanes and tornadoes.
Could these be warnings from God
For America to repent and return to Him?
Or just chance, part of a huge El Nino?
Either way, would it hurt to pray?

Why do we helplessly merely mourn the sins
That overwhelm our nation and our media?
We are God's people, Christ's body,
Called and equipped to win the victory
Over the world, the flesh, and the devil.
We are not merely ten thousand strong,
But millions, and growing.
We have been granted access to the Father
Who promises that the "fervent prayers
Of a righteous man avail much."

It's time to pray, not wring our hands.
We need serious, dedicated, fervent prayer.
Christians, pray for America!
Pray for our leaders in Congress,
And for the weak men of God to rise up.
In God's army, one can overcome a thousand,
And ten, ten thousand.
Why do we sit watching TV? Vote! Work!
And pray! America, it's time to pray.

Chapter X

Do We Really Go from Time into Eternity?

1. Time-Setters

The spin of the earth sets the time for the day,
The path of the moon makes the month.
The tilt of the earth sets the seasons,
Its orbit the length of the year.
The sun's life limits the time of our earth,
The stars measure eons of time—
Is it really so?

Earth, do you imagine that with your rotations
You make the days?
Moon, do you imagine that by your orbit
You measure the months?
Sun, do you imagine that your swinging
The earth in orbit makes the year?
And that you control the existence and span
Of the earth's life?
Stars, do you foolishly imagine
That you are the master of eons and ages?

He Who created Time and Eternity
Controls its every rhythm,
And He upholds all things
With the power of His Word,
Just as in the beginning He created them.
He is the Light of the sun and its power.
He is the Light of the world and its Lord and Life.
He is the destroyer of sin and death—and time—
When in His good will His plan is completed.
He is, before time began, after its end,
Lord of eternity.

2. When Time Stops for Me

When Time stops for me,
When I slip from Time into Eternity,
May I be walking in the Light,
Not groping in the dark of night;
For where that instant finds me,
I shall be throughout Eternity.

Praise God, pure Light,
Where Time stands still!
Praise Jesus, Light of the World,
Obedient to His will!
Thank God, Who made the Way
To plant His Light in us today.

Hallelujah, we are part of Him!
In Him we are the Light of the World!
In Him we have eternal life.
God's Light, which is eternity,
Creates eternity in me.

3. God's Day

You tell us in Your Word, Dear Lord,
That a thousand years is as a day.
From the perspective of eternity,
Does it just seem that way?

Or, at the speed of Light unchanging,
Does Time accelerate?
Or, rather, have You slowed time down
So life on earth can tolerate?

If we could come close to Light's speed
And travel but a day,
Computers figure when we return
A thousand years would have passed away.

Two thousand years would be two days,
A lifetime lived from two to noon.
In these terms, You do not tarry long.
Even so, Lord Jesus, come back soon.

4. In Two Millenia

In two millenia, two thousand years, Y2K,
Or just two days,
What have we, God's people, won
For the kingdom of our Lord?
How far has the good news spread?
How many souls have believed His Word?

The headlines shout of violence,
Scattered bombs of hate around the world,
Earthquakes, tornadoes, famine and floods,
And politics, quenching God's Word.

But God claims victory, not defeat:
Despite tyranny, the whispered Gospel's spread:
The Holy Spirit sparks revival flames.
In thousands of languages the Word is read.

God's victory is on the way.
We strive in vain to guess the time,
But His secret schedule is right on course
In His powerful, majestic hands, not mine.

5. One Moment

One moment in time reversed our world's trend,
Filtered out all but One, beginning and end.
Before, all were lost, stumbling in sin;
After, all who will, live eternally in Him.

6. Eternal Love Is Now

Once God so loved the world
That He gave His only begotten Son
That whosoever believeth in Him
Might be saved. It is done.

Yet the love of God is shed abroad
On our hearts always, every day,
And the gift of His Son is eternal;
He is still Salvation's Way.

God's love is always here and now,
Meeting our ever-present need,
As great as it was there and then
When He planted salvation's seed.

7. Memories without Limits

As we downsize our lifetime treasures
To fit into our homes for these days,
We need not discard a single one
Of the memories gathered along all our ways.

A song can bring back childhood games
Or a waltz in a loved one's arms.
A vase pictures our childhood home,
Or a foreign post with its charms.

All time is open to memory,
Any place comes into memory's view.
Each loved one can visit at our call,
And happy times live again in our minds, too.

8. Time Has No Forever

Time has no forever.
It marches inexorably from beginning to end.
Only in Eternity is there a forever.

Man has a Time and a forever.
Conceived and born in Time,
He is eternal, in the image of His Creator.
For each of us, Time is a passageway,
A maze with perplexing choices,
And a trap door exit into Eternity.

But which Eternity? For there are two.
Our Creator has given us a choice,
So that each man may determine in Time
Which Eternity is his.
God created us to share Eternity with Him,
But we must choose, and He will not force us.

If we seek Him, we have a Guide,
A Lamp unto our feet.
God loves us, calls us, entreats us
To choose His Way.

When we choose Jesus as the Way,
He leads us, protects us, guides us, encourages us.
He gives us His joy, His wisdom, His love.
We are born again with a new, eternal spirit,
Placed in Christ, forgiven, adopted by God.
His Holy Spirit comes to live within us,
And here in Time we begin to live forever,
In God's Eternity.

If we reject God's Way,
We will one day enter an Eternity
Prepared for those who choose the dark.

Time is the place of choice of our Forever—
Either with God in His Eternity,
Or without God along with men and angels
Who have chosen to disobey His laws,
To disdain His love, and reject their Creator.

Time has no forever,
But for each of us,
Forever begins in Time.

9. Beyond the Speed of Light

Beyond the speed of light,
Who can measure distance?
Who can measure Time?
Is there a distance so far
That numbers cannot comprehend
The stretch of light years,
And that Light itself fails the distance?

What measure can man use
Beyond the speed of Light?
Is there some swifter entity?
Or do we break through
Into negative years of Light
That lead to—what?
To the beginning?
Or some kind of circle of Time?

Or does Light set the limits?
Beyond the speed of Light,
Is there Eternity?
Beyond the light years,
Is there infinity?
Or in our search for limits,
Do we discover the Truth
Proclaimed in the Eternal Word
That the infinite God is Light?

10. A Flicker in Time

God is Light; Eternity is Light,
With everything less than the speed of Light
In Time, growing old, dying.
Does everything faster than Light go backwards?
God is the Master of Time, Eternal, Timeless,
But He reaches into Time with love—
For God is Love—
To readjust our lives with a miracle here and there,
A pushing back of Time, perhaps,
A flicker to make a tumor disappear.

11. Forever

Forever.
I'll live Forever.
Because I believe in Jesus
As my Lord and Savior, He gives me life
Eternal.

12. Time Out

Time out today—
Little work or play.
Sometimes I must catch up with me,
And find myself in my poetry.

13. The First Day of Forever

In precious moments of exquisite joy,
When praise and prayer, worship and adoration
Lead me into the presence of the Lord,
Time and space, and even I, myself melt
Into the infinite, eternal essence of my Lord,
And I am one with Him.

I wonder about, after my last day in Time,
My first moment of Eternity.
Shall I come before my Lord.
Totally aware of my every weakness, every failure,
Every willful turning away from His will,
Every unkind word or thought?
Surely I would fall down before Him,
My head at His feet,
But would He not lift me,
Turn up my face,
And let His eyes of flame
Burn from my heart and soul

Every spot and wrinkle?
Then into my purified spirit and soul
Would not His loving eyes
Pour in His joy and peace
Until my spirit heart would overflow?

But maybe there is even more!
Would His mind fill mine
Until my thoughts, my will, my faith
Are one with His?
Would He fill me with His Word, His wisdom
Until there are no more questions,
Only harmony with Him,
That oneness that is fullness of joy?
That infinite, eternal oneness,
I in Him and He in me,
Completely one, and one with all
Who are one with Him?

Wherever He will ask me to serve Him
In His infinite universe—far, far,
Or singing praises in the heavenly choir,
Or worshipping in the presence
Of our Lord God Almighty,
Or sitting at His feet as He teaches,
Will not my Lord and I be one,
His joy in me,
His overwhelming, infinite, eternal joy?

How will I be able to hold
Such wondrous, infinite, eternal joy?
Surely it will explode in praise,
In worship and adoration
To my Lord and God.

14. When Jesus Says, "It's Time."

"It's time," our Jesus said. "Come with me.
You've finished the work I've given you to do:
Planted the seed of my Word in fertile souls;
Scattered blossoms of my love to souls in need;
Helped those I placed in your path,
And raised physical and spiritual children,
Nurtured in My Word.

"It's time to leave behind the unfinished tasks.
(I have already reassigned them.)
To remove the useless burdens you are carrying;
(How light and bright you'll feel without the dross.)
It's time to let the gold and gems in you sparkle
(These are treasures you have laid up in heaven.)
It's time to show you the peace above understanding,
The love that has no limits.
It's time for Me to show you
The home I've prepared for you in heaven,
And take you to the Father in His glory."

My loved one says, "Don't mourn for me!
I'm home and happy with my Lord.
Celebrate the life God gave me
To share with you, each loved one, each friend.
I've left parts of me in and with you.
Rejoice! Celebrate!
And then plant your seeds and scatter your love
So that when it's time
Our Lord will bring you to be with us
In heaven."

Lord, may I be ready when you come to say,
"It's time."

15. Landmarks

Across the plains of years
High mountain tops of Truth
Stand strong against the clouds of change,
Reflecting the first light and lingering glow
In a darkening world:
Landmarks along the way.

In the valley of my childhood,
They were simply there,
With no names, no wonder, no questions.
But the knowledge of my college years
Clouded my view, polluted the air,
And there were no landmarks,
Not even a way or destination.

What joy when my exploring, searching heart
Recognized the mountain top of Light,
That unassailable Truth: "God is."
He was, and is, and will forever be,
Eternal mountain, immutable rock, goal, Light.
Landmark.

And standing near I found
Another peak called Right,
Unchanging above the drifting clouds,
Solid, without confusions or compromise,
No quicksand of deception,
No avalanche-prone gravel slopes,
But an eternal standard for our hearts,
Landmark of the Way.

And, oh, that lovely peak of Love!
God loves me, even me, just as I am—
So, so loved me that He gave His Son

To pay the penalty for sin,
To wash me in His blood,
To create in me a new heart,
So that He can receive me as His own
To fellowship with Him forever.
The eternal Truth of God's love for man,
Man's redemption planned before Time began,
Will lead us to our eternal home.
What a mountaintop! The one true God as man
Was a substitute on the cross for me;
He defeated sin and death
With His resurrection and eternal life.
Landmark!

Inside my Lord, eternally alive in Him,
What awesome peaks I find!
One rocky mountain, the Living Word,
Rises high above the smoke screen of the foe:
It flashes Light on every mountain peak,
And lights the Way in darkest night
And in the deepest valley with His Truth.
With His knowledge and Wisdom,
He blasts away all doubt and fear the enemy blows in.
To the gently glowing peaks of Love and Light
He adds the flowing Living Water,
Nourishing on slopes of prepared soil
The Living Word and Promises
That strengthen, correct, and protect faith,
And lead the Way to confidence and victory.

Lord, the world can be a dark and fearsome place,
Or lovely beyond imagination, filled with joy.
The difference is the Way; the Way is You.
When we find You, and in You find the Way,
Your landmark mountain peaks
Guide and keep us on the Way to Your Eternity.

16. Tapestry of Time

How far back, how far ahead
The shadow of the cross,
The reflection of the resurrected Light!
From Eden to New Jerusalem
All Time flows from that moment
When, after "It is finished,"
Our Savior God in Recreated Man,
Forever broke the bonds of sin and death
For all who, in faith, anticipated,
For all who, in faith, accept.

How patiently our Triune God planned
The tapestry of Time
With bits of shadow color from the cross,
With sparkles of resurrected Light
In every has-been or to-be age,
With wondrous parallel motifs—
Across space and time,
In things and events,
In places and people,
In lambs and lions,
Serpents and donkeys,
Fire, wind, and water,
Mountains and manna,
Trees and flowers,
Fruit and grain,
In threes and forties,
Sevens and seventies,
In bread and blood,
Wine and oil;
In tabernacle and temple,
Sinai and Jerusalem,
Red Sea and Jordan,
Canaan and Egypt,
Bethlehem and Galilee,

In Noah and Johab,
Abraham and Isaac,
Joseph and Moses,
Malchizedek and Aaron,
Joshua and David.
Every place and part of that perfect Life
Is pre-pictured and projected
In that tapestry of Time,
Eternalized in the Written Word.

As we walk the Tapestry of Time,
How precious to watch familiar patterns
From the Eternal Word unwind beneath our feet!
How precious to know,
As we know the Living Word,
That soon, after the seven dark bands,
The shadow colors of tribulation,
And the thousand-wide bright border of Light,
We'll see the Tapestry of Time
Roll up and vanish, leaving in Eternity
The Written, Living Word
In the Jewel of the New Jerusalem
Set in the new heavens and earth,
A record of Time for all eternity.

17. Birthdays Forever

Angels and shepherds were the first
To celebrate our Savior's birth;
A solemn joy, his birthday thirty,
Of age to start His ministry.
Disciples with love amid praise and strife
Honored Him at thirty-three years of life.
But by thirty-four, after utter dismay,
Unspeakable joy had come to stay,
For the resurrected, eternal, living Lord
Was in heaven building His church with His Word.

Two thousand plus we celebrate this year,
With our Savior, Lord, and Kin in us Here;
But one year, perhaps soon,
We'll praise Him in heaven
While those who denied Him
Have tribulation for seven.
A thousand more birthdays we'll have to praise
The King's earthly rule, in peaceful days.
Will, in righteous relief, Our Savior and His own
Mark that year He judged sinners
On the great white throne?

When the New Jerusalem, our eternal home,
Comes down from heaven as God Almighty's throne,
There'll be so much to celebrate day after days,
We'll praise and worship God forever, in all ways.

18. Celebrate Forever!

Do the angels celebrate His birth
With the saints around the throne?
With praise for prophesies fulfilled
And for those who are still His own?

In their songs of thanks and praise
For redemption of His man,
Does awe inspire a breathless hush
At the grandeur of God's bold plan?
Can we imagine ourselves in eternity
Gathered around the throne
With myriads of God's children
Thanking Him that we are His own?

Let's picture ourselves in eternity
With overflowing joy and praise
Where we can celebrate ceaselessly
And Christmas anthems raise.

Chapter XI

Lord, Do You Enjoy Our Songs, Praise and Worship?

1. The Wonder Of Your Presence

Lord, the wonder of Your presence
And Your magnificence overwhelm me.
I am immersed in awareness of Your glory.
Your love pours over me in rainbows of color.
Oh, that I would be able to share
The wonder of Your presence!

2. Hallelujah Day (Song)

Hallelujah, Hallelujah, Hallelujah, Lord!
Today is a Hallelujah Day.
The sun is bright, my heart is light,
For You are by my side.
Today is a Hallelujah Day.

My heart can sing because You're King,
Your Words in me abide.
Today is a Hallelujah Day.
Oh Hallelujah, Hallelujah, Hallelujah, Lord,
You're the Way to a Hallelujah Day.
Every Day is a Hallelujah Day.

3."Plenty Too Much"

The sky is oh so blue today,
The sun, warming my back,
Layers gold on tree trunk and leaves,
In glorious contrast to purple shadows.
A squirrel runs in waves across the grass
And scampers up a tree to the tip of a branch
As if to say, "I dare you to try this."
In every corner bright flowers seem to smile,
Delighting in the perfection of God's sunny day.
Each friendly face shares in the smiles.
Is that You, Lord, smiling at me?
Thank You, "Plenty too much."

Later, soft rain fills the sky
And sprinkles my face with cooling drops.
The trees flutter their leaves as if applauding.
This summer was blessed with rain
And the trees, which last year struggled to survive,
Stretch out to boast their growth
And revel in the fullness of their branches,
Knowing their roots are strong and full.
What a blessing is the rain!
Thank You, Lord, "Plenty too much."

And when, dear Lord, You give me glimpses
Of the many wondrous facets of Your love,
Of the intricate planning of the systems
As small as DNA, as large as the universe,
Of the wisdom and Truth of Your amazing Word,
Your willingness to take us as we are
And, gently, if we will, or sometimes harshly,
Lead us step by step into Your likeness,
Accepting us into Your heaven as Your children,
I thank You, Lord, "Plenty too much."

4. He Watches Over Me (Song)

Although I know I don't deserve it,
He watches over me, He watches over me.
Even when I'm thoughtless or even careless,
He watches over me with love.

(Chorus) With love, with love,
He watches over me, He watches over me,
With love, with love,
My Father watches over me with love.

His angel is near me, protecting and guiding:
He watches over me, He watches over me.
His Holy Spirit in me is teaching, providing,
He watches over me with love. (Chorus)

His Word abiding in me is my sword and my shield.
He watches over me, He watches over me.
I'm in Jesus; He's in me, and He is the Way.
He watches over me with love. (Chorus)

Because Jesus is my Savior and my Lord,
He watches over me, He watches over me.
He's given me His Name, and called me righteous.
He watches over me in love. (Chorus)

5. God's Armor (Song)

Start out each day with the Lord;
Put His wondrous armor on too:
The helmet of salvation
For you, His new creation.
Praise Your heavenly Father as you do.

The breastplate of His righteousness is next;
Just for being in Him it is your gift.
        Then fasten it with Truth—
        You know His Word is Truth—
Wear your gospel of peace shoes for a lift.

Pick up your trusty shield of Faith;
With your hearing of God's Word make it strong
        So it can withstand the darts
        Of Satan's cunning arts,
And it will protect you though the struggle's long.

Your weapon is God's Word, a two-edged sword;
Learn to use it as our Lord showed us how:
        Speak it clear and loud;
        Satan will be cowed.
He can't ever stand against God's living Word.

Now you are ready to stand,
Ready with His shield in your hand,
        Knowing He is in you,
        Able to defend you,
Proclaim God's Living Word, and stand, stand, stand.

6. Where is Your Trust (Song)

Some men trust in atom bombs,
And some men trust in tanks and planes,
But I will trust in the power of the Lord my God.

Some men trust in politics,
And some men trust in dirty tricks,
But I will trust in the power of the Lord my God.

Some men trust in dollar bills,
And some men trust in little pills,
But I will trust in the power of the Lord my God.

Some men trust in their good deeds,
And some men trust in philanthropies,
But I will trust in the power of the Lord my God.

Some men trust in oil wells,
And some men trust in their own selves,
But I will trust in the power of the Lord my God.

Some men trust in how-to books,
And some men trust in handsome looks,
But I will trust in the power of the Lord my God.

Some men trust in piles of things,
And some men trust in church and sings,
But I will trust in the power of the Lord my God.

7. For He Is Worthy

Give praise unto the Lord,
For He is worthy.
He has created a wonderful world.
Praise Him for His mighty works.
Praise Him for His Word,
Which endures forever.
Praise Him for His love
Which is without limit,
Praise Him for His mercy
For He forgives us our sin.
Praise Him for His presence
For he never leaves those who trust and love Him.

Praise Him for His righteousness.
Thank Him for His Son
Who has come to earth and lived and died
To bring us to our heavenly Father
Clothed in His righteousness.
All praise to the Lord,
For He is worthy.

8. Hosanna Hallelujah

Hosanna to the King, the people shout,
Laying palm leaves for His path.
Born to be King, He makes His claim
In sad, quiet dignity.
He knows that His task to save us all
By dying for our sins on Passover
Will change the cheers to jeers.
But in God's time, He will be King of all.
For He will conquer death, and rise
And those of us for whom He died
Will live forever with our Savior King,
And with our Father in heaven.
He died for us—and He's alive!
Hallelujah!

9. Ever-Existent (Song)

You—are—the—pre-existent,
The post-existent,
The ever-existent God,
Essence of Life,
Eternal life,
And You've given us life forever

With—You—the—pre-existent,
The post-existent,
The ever-existent God
Who sent His Son
To make us one
With that ever-existent Son.

10. Wonderful (Song)

Wonderful, wonderful, wonderful, wonderful,
Lord God Almighty.
Marvelous, marvelous, marvelous, marvelous,
Beyond our knowing.
Merciful, merciful, merciful, merciful,
Our loving Father.
Righteous, yes righteous, oh righteous, so righteous,
The Lord our God.

11. Safe for Eternity

While I'm praying for your healing,
For freedom from pain,
For God's love to enfold you,
Peace and joy remain,
I know you are safe in Jesus,
His for all eternity.
His strength and love are in you—
Your faith has set you free.

12. World Day of Prayer

All around the world today,
Your children, Lord, share in prayer.
What shall we ask, in groups or one by one,
But always in You, aware You are there?

Shall we ask for peace as the world sees peace?
Futile prayers, for no Way but You, Lord,
Can still the greed and hate and strife
Until Your kingdom's established in this world.

For food and clothes, every need met?
Of course, we pray for our daily bread,
Our, every one of us united as one
In Your body—that's the prayer You said.

Your will be done, that prayer's complete,
For Your will is always just,
And more, with love and mercy filled.
Always, in You we can trust.

13. Praise Your Holy Name, Lord (Song)

Praise Your Holy Name, Lord,
Praise Your Holy Name.
I'll take a little moment now
To praise Your Holy Name.
Praise Your Holy Name, Lord,
Praise Your Holy Name.
Thank You for this moment now
To praise Your Holy Name.

Praise Your Holy Name, Lord,
Praise Your Holy name.
You've given me this lovely day
To praise Your Holy Name.
Praise Your Holy Name, Lord,
Praise Your Holy Name.
Thank you for today, Lord,
To praise Your Holy Name.

Praise Your Holy Name, Lord,
Praise Your Holy Name.
You've given me this lifetime
To praise Your Holy Name.
Praise Your Holy Name, Lord,
Praise Your Holy Name.
Thank You for this lifetime
To praise Your Holy Name.

Praise Your Holy Name, Lord,
Praise Your Holy Name.
You've given me eternity
To praise Your Holy Name.
Praise Your Holy Name, Lord,
Praise Your Holy Name.
Thank You for eternity
To praise Your Holy Name.

14. A Psalm of Thanksgiving

This day and always will I rejoice
And thank and praise the Lord,
For He has chosen me;
He has called me to be His own.
I will enter His courts with praise.
He has forgiven all my sins;
He has cleansed me of all iniquity,
And placed me in His Son
And given me love, joy and peace.
His Holy Spirit fills me to overflowing,
And empowers me, because I believe in Him.
Before me, like a garden, are spread His promises.
In His grace He extends His hand
To lift me from my troubles.
There is no end to His mercy, no end to His love.

He leads me to live in pleasant places;
In the morning, my loved one beside me,
I awaken warm and secure.
Rainbows adorn my morning worship,
And decorate my breakfast table.
Abundant fruit in delicious, delightful variety,
Is spread before me.
In this world, He has blessed me in overflowing measure,
And in heavenly places, with all spiritual blessings.

With loving children, good and wise,
Has He blessed me,
And our grandsons grow
Like trees planted beside living waters.
They are chosen vessels who will choose the Lord,
Who will walk in His ways all the days of their lives,
And together we will worship Him throughout eternity.

With loving friends He has favored me.
With great joy we praise and worship,
And learn His Word and His mysteries.
His light and His love flow between us and through us,
And touch all He brings in our paths
With His love, His truth, His Light, His righteousness.
Our enemies are beneath our feet
Because we are in Christ Who is victorious.
His angels watch over us.
With health and long life has He blessed us
Because we trust in Him.

I hear His voice and quickly obey,
For He knows the Way, and His will is my delight.
I am in Him and He is in me,
And He will never leave me.
I serve Him with gladness and confidence.

His Word Have I hid in my heart,
And on it do I meditate day and night.
His wisdom is mine for the asking;
His Name is mine.
I am His candle, and His Light will I not hide.

In thanksgiving will I praise the Lord
All the days of my life,
And spread with persistent love and faith
The Gospel of salvation and love
Wherever He sends me.
The Lord is my Life.
In thankfulness and in faith
Will I serve and praise Him
Every day that I live, here and in eternity.

15. How Precious (Song)

How precious are Your children, Lord,
Hallelujah, Hallelu!
Chosen before Time began,
Hallelu!

How precious are Your children Lord,
Hallelujah, Hallelu!
Our salvation Your eternal plan,
Hallelu!

How precious are Your children, Lord,
Hallelujah, Hallelu!
For us You came to earth as man,
Hallelu!

. . . Perfect, You lived to show the Way . . .
. . . You died for us that awesome day . . .
. . . You live within our hearts today . . .

. . . Your Spirit lives within to teach . . .
. . . Through Him you commune in prayer with each . . .
. . . He gives us power the world to reach . . .

. . . We live to serve You, Lord, and praise . . .
. . . We thank You for Your love and grace . . .
. . . You give us eternity to praise,
Hallelu!

16. Prayer

Oh God, Almighty God,
Speak to me through Your Word.
Yielded, I learn of Your requirements:
You utterly abhor unrighteousness;
You totally reject empty words,
Surface sacrifices and ceremonies.
You tell us to come as little children,
Open, trusting, with clean hearts.

Oh Jehovah, with bowed head, closed eyes,
I kneel at Your feet.
Even through my closed eyes,
Your glory overwhelms me.
If I open my eyes, I see ground,
But with yielded Spirit I recognize You;
With my heart I know Your awesome greatness.
I am overwhelmed with Your power,
Fearful of Your righteousness,
Aware of my disobedience—

Oh Lord, my will is to obey.
I am so sorry I wander from Your perfect will.
I love You and worship You.

Because I know You are, there is no life without You.
Forgive me for dishonoring Your trust;
Thank You for giving me a way back.
O Jesus, Son of God, Lord of my life,
Forgive me. Lift my sins from me.
So much, O Lord, you bear!
All praise to the One Who can do all things!
In faith I ask, and it is done.
All thanks and praise and love to You.

You touch me, Lord Jesus,
And Your love flows over me and into me.
One drop of Your precious blood
Cleanses me of all sin,
Free to love and kneel in the very presence
Of our Lord God Almighty,
Creator of heaven and earth;
For You, Lord Jesus, have taken Your cloak,
Your shining white cloak of righteousness,
And wrapped it around my shoulders.
You bring me into the presence of Our Father,
Your love surrounding me; His love filling me.

Dear Father, I release my spirit.
I invite Your Holy Spirit within me
To pour out to you needs and yearnings,
Confessions and petitions too deep to know,
And to instruct me, correct me, inspire and guide me.

I listen, Dear Father, all Yours, yielded and ready.
I have no need that You will not provide,
For You care for me, Your child.
Your will is better for me than mine;
You have showered me with blessings;
Thank You for each one.
You have disciplined me, showing Your love.

Thank You for this day, O Lord.
I give it back to You in service.
As Your new creation, I abide in You,
Willing to learn and grow,
Eager to serve in little household tasks,
Or as a channel of Your Word and Love,
Committed to praise You without ceasing,
To meditate on Your Word,
To intercede for those You love.

Be glorified this day, O Lord,
In everything Your servant does.
I ask this in Jesus' glorious name,
For He is the Way You have provided. Amen.

17. Caring

I pick up my prayer list and sigh—
One hundred and five names.
One hundred and five people, families,
In need of healing, of love, of comfort,
In need of assurance of God's presence,
Of Christ's love and caring,
Of the Holy Spirit's guidance.

I add the leaders of our nation, our church and our pastors,
My family, my dear friends . . .
The Body of Christ throughout the world,
Those imprisoned behind the Iron or Bamboo Curtain,
Treasuring their page of Scripture:
Those starving in Asia and Africa,
In prison, dying ignorant of God,
Those in their search for righteousness
Following false cults and gods and heresies;
My neighbors . . . evangelists . . . missionaries . . .
Lord, I care, but the magnitude of my prayer list

Overwhelms me.
Were I to pray without ceasing for Your loving concern
For all those for whom I care,
I could not lift them all up to You.

And then, Oh Lord God Almighty,
I want to pray for You,
For Your caring is infinite.
You sent Your only Son
To bear the infinite sin of humanity
The crushing sins of each of us,
To suffer the illness of each and all;
Even knowing the glorious end,
How You must have suffered to see Him suffer so,
To see mankind, each of us whom You love,
Adding our nail or thorn or lash to tear His flesh.
And still You love us,
Sending Your Holy Spirit to indwell our rescued souls,
To guide, teach, admonish—
So patient is Your love, Oh God!
How long Your prayer list
As Jesus by your side points out this one and that,
And even me.
You know the needs, the longings and pain
Of every one of us, Your children,
Every thought and doubt and desire,
And You care.
Even though You are in control,
You want us to care, too, and pray.
My list, Oh God is so infinitesimal a part
Of Your list, and You are praying for each one, too.

Dear Father, in Jesus' name I lift up to you . . .

About the Author

Katherine Ropiequet, born in St. Louis, raised in Illinois, started writing poems when she was six and has been writing ever since. After an AB and a BS from the University of Illinois and an MA in Creative Writing at the State University of Iowa, Katherine (Kit) taught high school English until her college sweetheart, Lloyd J. Inman asked her to be his war bride. While Lloyd was in Italy charging the Gothic Line, Kit worked as a claim adjuster in Workmen's Compensation, and tucked in lessons in oil painting.

After the war, Kit concentrated on being an active Army Officer's Wife and mother of three boys, with 25 moves in 29 years, including two tours in Heidelberg, Germany. Whenever convenient, she indulged her irrepressible love of teaching, the last six years college English. Intending to write children's stories to inspire as well as entertain, Kit took the Institute of Children's Literature writing course, and wrote a number of short stories. But after being filled with the Spirit, she focused her teaching on Bible Studies and Sunday School, adding teaching beginners oil painting as outreach.

All these years, Kit was writing poetry and researching and preparing in-depth Bible studies. Many of her poems were published in magazines, and, to share her faith with her many friends, Kit self-published three books of poetry and her book of memories. These friends have urged her to seek a wider distribution of this collection of poems about her growing awareness and knowledge of our wonderful God.

Other Books by

Katherine R. Inman

God Is Like That

Poems and meditations on the nature of God, illustrated with drawings by the author.

Joy to Share

Booklet of poems about joy for enclosure in Christmas cards.

When You Pray . . .

Poems and meditations on "The Lord's Prayer."

Study Notes and Questions on Books of the Bible

Twelve Studies: The Gospel of John, Ephesians, Philippians, Colossians, The Revelation of John, Daniel, I and II Thessalonians, James, I and II Peter, Hebrews, Joel, Jude

Here It Comes Again, Wonderful Christmas

Fifty-eight years of Christmas poems.

My Memory Book

Informal memories of a remarkable family and 82 wonderful years during a century of change.

18. Thanksgiving Prayer for our Nation

Our Father Who art in heaven,
We thank You for the many blessings
You have granted us, Your nation.

Forgive us for taking for granted
    The freedom, so precious and so gallantly won.
    The peace and protection we have enjoyed
        for so many years,
    And the prosperity,
All made possible
    By the Constitution Your Word inspired,
    By our commitment to be one nation under God,
    And by Your never-failing love.

We thank You
    That when we came under terrorist attack,
    Even in our fear and anger,
    We found the faith to turn to You.
    We are especially thankful
    That we can depend on Your Word and promises
    To help us stand firm until You lead us
        In establishing safety and freedom from fear
        Not only for America
        But for all nations of good will.
For the blessings of being
        Loved
        Forgiven
        And called to be Your people,
    We are truly grateful.

We ask for Your protection, guidance, and help
    In the struggle for the right.

In the precious name of our Lord, Jesus, Amen.